KT-564-864

cooking in
provence

ACKNOWLEDGEMENTS

Alex

To Jess with all my love for all your love and support.

Special thanks to Pete and Di for their great friendship, for being the most
wonderful photographer and stylist to work with and, not least,
for putting up with me every summer.
Thanks to my editor Susan Fleming; Mum; Raymond Blanc for the huge part he's
played in my career; my assistants at Le Baou, Mary and Florence; Heather, Juliana
and Bryone at Headline; Fiona at Pike; my suppliers Jacky, Doume and Bruno
for their glorious produce and my agents Tony, Anne and Pete.
Lastly, thanks to all of our guests and friends at Le Baou d'Infer who have tried,
tested and tasted all of these recipes with bubbling enthusiasm and
barrels of laughter while living and cooking in Provence.

Peter

This is the easy part: saying thank you to everyone who helped in making
this book a reality. Easier still is saying a special thank you to Diana
who has made this corner of Provence so special.
The hard part is having to cope with all those endless days of glorious sunshine.
Harder still is having to eat all the wonderful meals Alex is able to invent
with such evident skill and *laissez-faire*.

cooking in provence

Alex Mackay
with Peter Knab

headline

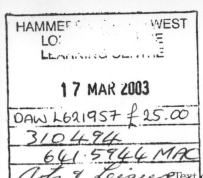

HAMMER⸱ ⸱ ⸱ WEST
LO⸱ ⸱ ⸱
LEARNING CENTRE

17 MAR 2003

DAW L621957 £25.00
310494
641.5944 MAC
Arts & Leisure

Text copyright ©2003 Alex Mackay
Photography copyright ©2003 Peter Knab

The right of Alex Mackay to be identified as the Author of the Work has
been asserted by him in accordance with the Copyright, Designs and
Patents Act 1988.

First published in 2003
by HEADLINE BOOK PUBLISHING

10 9 8 7 6 5 4 3 2 1

All rights reserved. No part of this publication may be reproduced, stored
in a retrieval system, or transmitted, in any form or by any means
without the prior written permission of the publisher, nor be otherwise
circulated in any form of binding or cover other than that in which it is
published and without a similar condition being imposed on the
subsequent purchaser.

Every effort has been made to trace and contact copyright holders of all
the materials in this book. The author and publisher will be glad to
rectify any omissions at the earliest opportunity.

Cataloguing in Publication Data is available from the British Library

ISBN 0 7472 4311 5

Design by Fiona Pike
Styling by Diana Knab

Typeset in Veljovic by Pike

Printed and bound in France by Imprimerie Pollina - n° L88521

HEADLINE BOOK PUBLISHING
A division of Hodder Headline
338 Euston Road
London NW1 3BH

www.headline.co.uk
www.hodderheadline.com

To find out more about the school visit www.lebaou.com

310494

Contents

FOREWORD BY DELIA SMITH

Alex Mackay is, first and foremost, a brilliant chef. Yet at the same time he's also much more than that. He has a quite rare and very special gift which goes beyond simply creating beautiful dishes. That gift is the ability to teach, inspire and enthuse others who want to learn how to cook creatively. This is something I personally admire a great deal and is why I have asked him to lead the food and wine workshops in the restaurants at my beloved Norwich City Football Club.

There is, though, another connection here, as Peter and Di Knab are two of my husband Michael's and my oldest friends, and we have watched with delight their dazzlingly beautiful house in deepest Provence being transformed into Le Baou d'Infer cookery school, and becoming an internationally famous centre of good food, wine and the warmest hospitality. Now added to all this is a very fine and beautiful cookery book indeed, which I am proud to present as a fitting tribute to all they have achieved.

Delia

LE BAOU D'INFER

I first met Peter and Diana Knab in 1995, when I was working at Le Manoir aux Quat' Saisons in Oxfordshire as the director of the cookery school there. While working with Raymond Blanc on *A Blanc Christmas*, I got to know the publishers' chosen photographer Peter Knab. We became close friends, and one evening, while listening to jazz in London's Soho, we hatched a plot that was to become Le Baou d'Infer cookery school. Peter and Di had holidayed at their house in Provence for several years, and were looking for an excuse to spend more time there. An Antipodean chef-teacher, young enough to be their son, could not have been a more unlikely part of that plan, but the seed was sown, the logistics discussed, and soon the house was being adapted to its new role.

We opened in 2000 and haven't looked back. Every course we've run has been full of people from around the world, including Australia, South Africa, America, Switzerland, Holland and Germany. Whether they cook every day or have never cooked before, they get caught up in the excitement and fun. Our guests become friends and the overriding impression throughout the summer is that of a house party with a never-ending stream of meals, conversation and laughter.

The days are long for Peter, Di and me but so much fun that time slips by unnoticed. I am never more alive than when I'm with our students, all of us in a happy and very noisy group, with pans, produce and ideas circling the room. It's sharing rather than teaching, talking about, touching, smelling and greedily tasting the ingredients and dishes. Peter is the head wine buyer and taster (the wine cellar is referred to as Pete's corner) and host. He has also become an ace barterer and cares passionately about quality. All our suppliers make sure they have the best produce available when he visits the daily market in Cogolin. They'll also quite happily stop the mid-morning traffic while loading up his car. Di is the busiest of us all. She never stops, be it banishing weeds from her huge and beautiful garden, keeping the house running or regaling us all with hilarious tales of her travelling days. At these, Peter will sometimes play the straight man and at others insist on slightly different versions of the wilder stories. The three of us are enjoying the great success that is Le Baou d'Infer. A fine result of what began as a casual conversation, and a success that continues in no small part due to the spirit and bounty of Provence, the beautiful region of France to which this book is devoted.

INTRODUCTION

Provence is an unparalleled feast for the senses, reflected in the azure blue of its sky and sea, in the stony hillsides fragrant with the scent of lavender and mountain thyme, and in the vibrant colours and exhilarating fresh flavours of the food. Softly lit languorous afternoons always draw me, waiting to dine in the shade of a richly leafed tree, sipping chilled local rosé and crunching on croûtons spread with rich, black tapenade. Or evenings by the sea, with laughter and little concern about the more serious side of life, tossing olive stones into the Med and waiting for a bouillabaisse to arrive. More often than not, on many of these occasions I'm elsewhere, hot and flustered, doing the actual cooking. But I'm just as happy in my beloved kitchen as I am anywhere else in Provence, where the ingredients are a source of permanent inspiration and pleasure.

Provence itself is divided up into six *départements*: Vaucluse, Bouches du Rhône, Alpes de Haute Provence, Hautes Alpes, Alpes Maritimes and our own region, the Var. Each 'department' offers its own culinary specialities, which may differ from other regions simply by the addition of a different herb, or just a bit more garlic, and there is much in the way of interdepartmental rivalry, each claiming dishes as their own. Provençal cooking is often referred to as *la cuisine du soleil*, 'the cuisine of the sun', and this sums it up pretty well, but not completely, as the cooler times, of which there are admittedly a lot less than in most places, have their own wonderful repertoire of dishes too.

The word 'Provençal' could describe a gentle, thoughtful way of moving through life, for passing time in a way that stretches conveniently at moments of pleasure and a little less so when you want the shutters fixed. Being part of Provençal life and becoming Provençal (and I think you really can, it's a state of mind) are wonderful things to aspire to. The people themselves may seem calm and unconcerned, but are actually the most passionate I know. An argument is always simmering somewhere. Just watch a seemingly innocent game of boules and you'll see what I mean. Most things are attacked, verbally at least, and when it comes to many workmen, verbally only, with fervent vigour.

Opinions are, mostly, there to have and hold for life, not to be changed, and from a culinary viewpoint certainly not by a lanky chap from the other side of the world. This is part of the Provençal charm. Monsieur, waiting in the fishmonger's in

Cogolin has always made his aïoli in a mortar and pestle. He is totally unimpressed by, even dismissive of, my whisk and bowl technique, no matter how practical it may be. Madame in La Mole heard I was a *cuisinier*. She wanted to show me a few things. 'Since I was *une petite fille, vous comprenez*,' she has cooked her *soupe au pistou* for hours rather than in the short fresh burst that I prefer. No matter what my argument, or the suggestion that being different is OK, a slightly pitying smile and famed Provençal shrug are all I'll get. As for bouillabaisse, well, that's another story (it is, later).

The Provençal way of being is reflected no more completely than in its food. To this day the seasons command more respect than in any other place where I have worked or visited.

Spring is the season of promise, the colours are soft and shy. The first of the tiny broad beans and peas make an appearance. The shiny, intensely green beans are shelled and eaten raw with salt and olive oil or the *bagna calda* of Nice, or sautéed with a little savory and served alongside cutlets of the first spring lamb. Peas are added to fresh *soupe au pistou*, or cooked, *à la française*, with carefully softened fresh white onions, lettuce and sometimes little artichokes. These have their first season in spring as well. The tender little buds are just trimmed – they have no choke to speak of – and all except the very outside leaves are edible so the preparation is easy. They are finely sliced and tossed with lemon and olive oil or cooked *à la barigoule*, a preparation with as many different versions as bouillabaisse.

Asparagus, wild and cultivated, also arrives in abundance in spring. The white, held in such high regard in northern France, is not so favoured in Provence. The violet-tipped green variety with only a tiny woody stem and tender flavoursome spears that need neither peeling nor trimming is the chosen delicacy. They are either blanched then roasted in olive oil, poached or steamed. Served in the Provençal way with olive oil and lemon juice to slide each each spear in before every bite, asparagus is one of spring's most sensual pleasures.

In spring, as during most of the year, markets bring individual treats that reach beyond their produce. An elderly woman sits proudly with her goat's cheese, each slightly imperfect round carefully topped with a sprig of mountain savory. She has just three trays. One has her freshest cheeses, which are pure white, creamy and mild enough to eat with berries and sugar. The second tray holds cheeses that are slightly dryer, yellowing a little and more strongly flavoured, but still creamy enough to be grilled and melted lusciously atop garlic-rubbed croûtons to serve in the midst of a salad dressed with olive oil and herbs. The third tray of cheese, dryer again, dark yellow and sweetly pungent, is to be eaten while sipping good red wine as a cheese course. She also offers a few bunches of wild savory, carefully tied with brown string, that surround her cheeses like a protective border. She may not have been at the market long but was probably up very early milking her goats. She shares half a roast chicken and a bottle of rosé wine with the monsieur next to her who is selling cured sausages and mountain-dried ham.

Another maker of goat's cheese once visited Pete and Di. She'd had a problem, caused I think by the mistral. Left without electricity, she'd come in search of some so she could milk her goats. They agreed to an exchange: electricity for cheese. Their power was hers to use at will and she milked away happily for weeks. But after the first few trays the promise of goat's cheese melted away...

With summer comes the food for which we know Provence best, when we rejoice at the arrival of sun-gorged tomatoes, peppers, aubergines and courgettes, the latter often with their bright yellow flowers still attached. It is the time to make ratatouille, Provence's most celebrated vegetable dish from which the scent of summer itself rises as it murmurs gently at the side of the stove. Gently and lovingly cooked, the ingredients are first sautéed separately, then cooked together with softened onions and garlic that melt sweetly into what I think is the tastiest of all vegetable dishes. Ratatouille makes an aromatic and robust partner for grilled fish, usually one of the many varieties of sea bream such as *marbré* or *pagre*, or lamb, often cooked outside, sometimes over a fire of vine leaves. It is also eaten cold. The rich cooking oil oozes on to your plate and provides the perfect excuse to finish the bread basket. Olives are sometimes added, and a generous scattering of basil offers a lovely burst of freshness.

One of the biggest treats in Provence is the stonefruit, picked when ripe and sold soon after. The joy of a perfect ripe peach is something special, still warm from the sun and so full of juice that it pours down your chin with each bite. There are huge piles of local berries on sale, too, including up to four types of strawberry – from the heavily scented *marais des bois* to the delicate pink *garigette*. Their sweet jam-like scent will permeate the entire market and drift down the street as the day warms up.

Of course for a visitor the most enjoyable thing is to become part of the local crowd, milling around with purpose, but always having time to talk. You are recognised by the *vendeurs* and *vendeuses*, who pull out the best titbits from behind the stalls. We have, on a much more regular basis than the weekly market, become very attached to and well served by one particular supplier: Jacky, our butcher. He is a *maître boucher* who considers himself, quite rightly, to be an artist. He never lets himself be hurried or flustered, but talks first of all very carefully about the recipe, finds the cut of lamb (in the case of a navarin, for example, the neck end, still on the bone, properly hung), then prepares it perfectly while you watch, not hesitating to give a little flourish with his knife where he thinks the flourish is merited. Then he wraps it with great care in pink-tinted paper proudly bearing the name of his family firm, above, naturally, the words *Maître Boucher*.

Life in Provence is not restricted to the summer days by the sea, and during those summer days the sea is perhaps best avoided, crowded as it is. And there is always the threat of the mistral, the legendary wind that blows through Provence. If it lasts for more than five days a husband has a legal right to kill his wife (or so I'm told; I'm not sure what happens the other way around). This wind has the ability to completely throw you, to make you annoyed and irritated; but the feeling it leaves, once passed, is one of cleansing and peace.

The autumn and winter countryside, like the cuisine, has an enrapturing spell all of its own. The food is powerfully flavoured, warming stews and daubes, roasted game birds, and vegetables not often associated with Provence, such as endives and sweet potatoes. The Provençal passion for the hunt is legendary, although the woods, like the sea, may offer less than they once did. Some of the traditional offerings are now so rare they are only eaten behind closed doors, but there are still boar, partridges, pheasants and woodcocks, the latter one of France's great delicacies. More common and commonly discussed are the many varieties of mushrooms, each of which has its place, not only to be found but used. Each mushrooming spot is jealously guarded. I took a flight over specially in late October one year so that Sylvain, the guardian of Peter's vines, could take us to a spot where he finds them on a regular basis. He found them in abundance, we feasted on them for days and a few of the recipes have made their way into the book.

These mushroom recipes, like a few others in this collection, are difficult for you to re-create outside of Provence. But they exist and, along with the azure blue of the sea and sky, they make up the inimitable, ever-changing spirit of Provence.

LES JARDINS DE PROVENCE

Provence is one huge and beautiful garden. The vegetables and fruit bask in the sunshine and ripen as they should, on their vines or trees. The freshness and abundance of vegetables is proudly displayed in weekly markets and in the many greengrocers which, at least for now, are still found in most village streets. My regular greengrocer, Bruno, has a great little shop in Cogolin with a boat in the middle of it that comes halfway out into the street. I'm not sure why, and for some reason have never asked; maybe it used to be a fishmonger's. In any case, the care which he and his four staff take with the vegetables and fruit and the beauty of his shop are astonishing.

On the right as you enter are carefully lined up aubergines, peppers, tomatoes and cucumbers, as well as red, white and yellow onions, garlic in plaits, and loose and huge banana shallots, most of which are larger than the onions. There are many different types of potatoes, and Bruno will be able to tell you what to use each for. The relative merits of Rattes and Grenailles for salad is a matter more for personal choice, but he'll happily scrape and cut a few in the shop so you can see and feel which have the firmest, yellow-tinted flesh. Big baskets of herbs, rocket and the mixture of tiny salad leaves known as *mesclun* run down the centre. Alongside these are great bunches of artichokes, their leaves tightly bunched and stalks carefully tied, and often up to five varieties of green beans. On the left there are all of the fruits. Figs – which have two seasons, first in spring and another that coincides with the harvest in September – sit in their paper wrappers like cupcakes, as do any of the more delicate and very ripe stone fruit. There is a big basket of lemons with their leaves still attached, which are knobbled, natural and richly scented. In Provençal folklore the lemon is said to fill you with the sun's energy. When added to your food it causes a bright, positive force to flow throughout and charge your body and mind. This is possibly why the basket is always half full!

Whichever vegetable or fruit there is an abundance of spills out on to trestle tables in the street, and is usually snatched up early as the price and quality reflect the height of the season. In July and August the boat, which is very pretty with blue and white stripes, is often full of piles of fat, juicy, bright red local tomatoes. None is perfectly formed but all are perfectly flavoured. There are also little pots of red and yellow cherry tomatoes still attached to their heavily scented vines and bursting with ripeness. For me, the true, sun-filled taste of these tomatoes is a massive part of the beauty of cooking and eating in Provence.

Wonderfully named *pomme d'amour* (I prefer this to the more common *tomate*), the tomato is my favourite of all ingredients. Especially when attached to its vine, rounded, plump and blushing bright red, this vegetable-fruit holds more sway over most Mediterranean cuisines than any other. Nowhere more so than in Provence, where it is involved in most of the famous dishes: it's added to bouillabaisse, it lifts and enriches a daube, and is a main ingredient in a *salade Niçoise*. But at the height of summer, they are best neither peeled nor seeded, just cored and cut, salted, left for half an hour or so, and eaten with olive oil and basil. It is also the perfect time to make tomato tarts, using a massive quantity of rich, densely coloured fruits which, cooked slowly, dry out and concentrate to a sweet sticky mass.

The vegetable dishes of Provence are often very simple. The main ingredient is majestically shown off, enhanced by a shower of herbs or a little lemon and olive oil; or by anchovies, salted or cured, and a few olives or tapenade. Much more than just accompaniments, vegetables stand out and sparkle in their own right. I'll often find myself having gone days without meat or fish because the vegetables on offer were so appealing. In this chapter there are recipes for everyday eating, dishes that are relatively quickly prepared and suit being either starters in a more formal meal, or a light lunch. Most of the dishes, particularly the salads, are perfect as part of a buffet. I love to eat this way: first of all trying a bit of each dish, next going back for a little more of your favourite. Then, relaxing and just grazing, spearing the last slice of aubergine with your fork, scooping up a courgette flower and dunking a bit of bread in the rich tomatoey olive oil that oozes out of the dish, sipping at another glass of wine, and whiling the afternoon or evening away.

For any such meal, as for any cuisine that concentrates on fresh and honest flavours, the high notes are provided by herbs. As you will notice throughout this book I have my favourites, notably basil, which I would cheerfully put with almost anything if not for the need for a little variety. In Provence herbs, wild and cultivated, fresh and dried, are treasured. Fresh, soft herbs such as basil are sold in enormous bunches or great pots the size of small trees (the thought of them always makes me want to get on a plane when I am buying half a dozen very expensive leaves at my local supermarket in Britain). The scent of herbs at any market-place is often so overpowering that you can follow your nose to piles of peppery basil and fragrant mint. Basil, parsley and mint are the most commonly used; chives are generally passed over for spring onions; chervil is not really robust enough for the Provençal palate but sometimes adds a little anise flavour to *mesclun* mixtures; and tarragon is generally restricted to Béarnaise. The most vital ingredient in the use of soft herbs is timing. They should always be added at the last possible moment. This way they give a wonderful fresh burst and their flavours are let loose by the contact with heat rather than being dulled and greyed by too much exposure to it.

Wild thyme, savory and rosemary are found all over the sun-beaten hillsides. They are cut, in bunches, already almost completely dry, and kept at the side of the oven to flavour slow-cooked dishes or to crumble into sauces and breadcrumbs. It is unexpectedly difficult, I have found, to get any of these herbs fresh during the summer. Savory, known in old dialect as *pebre d'ase* or 'ass's pepper', whether fresh or dried, is the most typical of Provençal herbs. Fresh, it is a perfect partner in spring for small beans and artichokes and is used fresh or dry throughout the year with lamb. I don't think I'd ever come across it before coming here. But now I add it to dishes with no restraint whatsoever. It will scent any stew or daube that I make, be included in all bouquets garnis, and I'll crumble it into herb breadcrumbs or infuse it in olive oil to braise or roast red peppers and courgettes. The stalks and fronds of wild fennel are widely used as well, mainly when baking or grilling whole fish, but they also make a good trivet to roast a leg of lamb on.

In spring and summer I love to make *soupe au pistou*. The vegetables I use often vary, as they should, depending on what catches my eye. It may be a bunch of carrots with their greens still attached, along with some little turnips and young leeks which have no woody centre and can be used complete, apart from the very tops. I'll take the best of the beans, young *fèves* if available, peas, thick string beans which I'll chop, or runners. I leave out the traditional pasta, and always make it with water. The clear, fresh flavour of the vegetables is only muddied by a chicken or meat stock.

Whenever I go to Bruno's shop he greets me with an enthusiasm that he somehow maintains throughout his six-and-a-half-day week. He'll take me around the shop telling me which fruit is best for the table, cutting off pieces of each with his little pocket knife, perhaps peaches or fat white nectarines, little greengages or figs. I once asked him for some tropical fruit and he was excitement itself, telling me that a box of rhubarb had just arrived. I made a very acceptable tart, but anything from too far away may not always suit the gardens and cuisine of Provence. Both of these are rooted in deep tradition and warm familiarity.

Soupe de Feves et Petits Pois
Pea and Broad Bean Soup

Perhaps because of their colour, perhaps for their sweetness, youth and vibrant sense of spring, these two vegetables are eagerly awaited. This soup, simply made with water rather than stock, which would only serve to confuse and distract from the bright fresh flavours, uses some of the pods as well. The pods should be added only if young, tender and unsprayed; if they're not, just add a third again of peas and beans. You absolutely must cook the soup as quickly as possible, adding more water if necessary, or you'll lose all that is so appealing about the flavour. A little mint, just added at the end, is the perfect finishing touch to the freshest of soups which bursts with the flavour of Provençal springtime.

For 4
400G (14OZ) FRESH PEAS IN THEIR PODS
500G (1LB 2OZ) FRESH YOUNG BROAD BEANS IN THEIR PODS
1 SMALL ONION, PEELED AND CHOPPED
4 GARLIC CLOVES, PEELED AND CHOPPED
100ML (3½FL OZ) OLIVE OIL
APPROX. 1 LITRE (1¾ PINTS) WATER
100ML (3½FL OZ) WHIPPING CREAM
1 SMALL BUNCH FRESH MINT, LEAVES PICKED FROM THE STALKS, SLICED

Shell the peas and broad beans, keeping the pods. Wash the latter well, then chop them into small pieces.

Sweat the chopped onion and garlic in the olive oil for about 2 minutes. Add the pea and bean pods, then sweat for a further 3 minutes until they are soft. Cover with the water then bring to the boil. Simmer rapidly for about 5 minutes, then add half of the peas and beans. Boil for a further 5 minutes, then purée and strain through a fine sieve.

Blanch the remainder of the peas and beans for 1 minute in boiling water, then add to the puréed soup along with the cream. Bring back to the boil, add the sliced mint, and serve.

AUBERGINE A LA MENTHE ET AUX PIMENTS
Aubergines with Mint and Chilli

When baking them, aubergines are like sponges, and will absorb as much good olive oil as you care to add, making them melting and almost pâté-like on the inside. They then need sharp and pronounced flavours to cut their richness: lemon, chilli and mint is a favoured combination.

FOR 4
2 LARGE AUBERGINES
80ML (3FL OZ) OLIVE OIL
JUICE OF 2 LARGE LEMONS, FINELY GRATED ZEST OF 1
SALT
1 SMALL MILD CHILLI, SEEDED AND FINELY CHOPPED
1 SMALL BUNCH FRESH MINT, LEAVES PICKED FROM THE STALKS, SLICED

PREHEAT YOUR OVEN TO 180°C/350°F/GAS 4.
Slice the aubergines thickly and lay the slices flat on a tray. Mix the olive oil and the juice of the first lemon and brush the aubergine slices with half of this. Turn them over and brush with the other half. Salt them well and bake for 15-20 minutes until the flesh is meltingly soft.

Sprinkle over the zest and juice of the second lemon, the chopped chilli and mint, and serve.

ON SALTING AUBERGINES
I find it unnecessary to salt aubergines as these days they are generally good and sweet. For me, this whole process leaves them rather tyre-like in texture.

POIVRONS BRAISES AUX OLIVES
Braised Peppers and Olives

Red, yellow and sometimes orange peppers brighten any market shelf. To be honest, although I can never resist mixing the colours, I think the red have the best, most natural flavour. Often partially green where they haven't completely ripened, some people leave them in the sun for a few days to finish them off, but I like them just as they are. When each one is individually shaped, bent and twisted, they are so full of flavour that when cut or broken they give off a powerful scent of chillies. This makes them very hard to skin, but as I become more of a cook and less of a chef I do this less often anyway.

The olives and anchovies add a bit of bite and are a very traditional accompaniment. You could also serve these with fresh mozzarella or goat's cheese and basil.

FOR 4
2 RED PEPPERS AND 2 YELLOW PEPPERS
SALT AND CAYENNE PEPPER
4 GARLIC CLOVES, PEELED
100ML (3½FL OZ) EXTRA VIRGIN OLIVE OIL
50ML (2FL OZ) RED WINE VINEGAR
50G (1¾OZ) ANCHOVIES
16 BLACK OLIVES, STONED
1 SMALL BUNCH FRESH FLAT-LEAF PARSLEY, LEAVES PICKED FROM THE STALKS

PREHEAT YOUR OVEN TO 190°C/375°F/GAS 5.
Cut each pepper in half lengthways, remove the seeds and cut them in half again. Lay them skin side up on a roasting tray, and season well. Press the garlic cloves lightly but don't crush them, and add to the peppers in the tray. Pour over the olive oil and vinegar, cover the tray with foil, and put it in the oven. Braise the peppers for 45 minutes until they are completely soft. Lift off the foil and transfer them to a bowl. Cover the bowl with clingfilm and leave for about 15 minutes.

Next skin the peppers, but if any of the skins are really stubborn don't worry too much. Just leave them, or you will end up with no peppers.

To finish the vinaigrette, remove the whole garlic cloves from the tray, and crush in a bowl. Whisk in the cooking juices, and season well with salt and cayenne pepper. Pour this over the roasted peppers and serve with the anchovies, olives and flat-leaf parsley.

SOUFFLE DE POIVRONS ROUGES
Twice-cooked Red Pepper Soufflé

Both cooks and guests adore these soufflés: the cooks because they can be prepared at least 12 hours in advance; and guests just enjoy the crispy coating and soft centre. Undercook them slightly during the first baking so that they puff and blow during the second. The red pepper chutney provides a sharp contrast, but you could just as easily serve the soufflés with an olive oil-dressed green salad or roasted vegetables.

FOR 4

1 VERY LARGE RED PEPPER, SEEDED

2 TBSP VEGETABLE OIL

SALT AND CAYENNE PEPPER

30G (1¼OZ) BUTTER, PLUS EXTRA, WELL SOFTENED, FOR THE MOULDS

2 TBSP PLAIN FLOUR

100ML (3½FL OZ) MILK

1 LARGE EGG YOLK, PLUS 3 EGG WHITES

100G (3½OZ) PROVENCAL BREADCRUMBS (SEE PAGE 31)

4 TBSP PISTOU (SEE PAGE 170), WITH PARMESAN

RED PEPPER CHUTNEY

2 LARGE RED PEPPERS, SEEDED AND SLICED INTO STRIPS

3 TBSP OLIVE OIL

50ML (2FL OZ) WATER

30ML (1FL OZ) RED WINE VINEGAR

1 TBSP HONEY

TO SERVE

1 SMALL BUNCH ROCKET

PREHEAT YOUR OVEN TO 190°C/375°F/GAS 5.

Roast the red pepper for the soufflé in the vegetable oil with a little salt and cayenne for half an hour, or until soft but not coloured. Transfer the pepper to a blender and blend until fine. Put the purée in a pan and reduce it over a high heat by about two-thirds, stirring constantly. Transfer to a bowl and set aside.

Melt the 30g butter in a small saucepan. Remove from the heat and stir in the flour until smooth. Still off the heat, stir in the milk and return to the heat. Bring the mixture to the boil (it should thicken enough to come away from the side of the pan) and add the red pepper purée. Transfer to a bowl, cool slightly and whisk in the egg yolk. Season well with salt and cayenne.

Line four ramekins well, first with some softened butter then some of the Provençal breadcrumbs. Sprinkle a few extra breadcrumbs into the bottom of the mould (which will eventually be the top of the soufflé) and set aside. You need a few breadcrumbs left over to finish the dish.

Whisk the egg whites to firm peaks then mix a third into the pepper mixture. This can be done quite briskly: the idea is to have the mixture similar in texture to the egg whites. Add this to the remaining egg white and fold gently to combine. Fill the lined ramekins with the soufflé mixture. Put a teaspoon of the pistou in the middle of each soufflé, pushing it down a little.

Place the ramekins into a bain-marie of hot water that reaches two-thirds of the way up the sides of the ramekins, and bake in the preheated oven for 8-10 minutes (the soufflés should still be slightly soft in the centres). Leave the soufflés to cool for a few minutes.

Spread the remaining breadcrumbs over a small oven tray. Remove the soufflés from their moulds, arrange them evenly spaced on top of the breadcrumbs, and set aside in a cool place for up to 12 hours (but not in the fridge).

Meanwhile, for the red pepper chutney, combine all the ingredients in a pan, cover and allow to simmer over a medium heat for 15 minutes until the peppers soften. Boil until the liquid is almost completely evaporated, remove from the heat, season with salt and cayenne, and set aside.

To serve, preheat your oven to 200°C/400°F/Gas 6, and cook the soufflés for 6 minutes until they puff up and get crusty on the outside.

Toss the red pepper chutney with the rocket and serve with the soufflés. Sprinkle any remaining crumbs over the top.

Fleurs de Courgettes Farcies aux Tomates
Stuffed Courgette Flowers with Tomatoes

I know they don't taste of an awful lot, but I can't resist using courgette flowers, for as far as I'm concerned they do their bit just by looking so glorious. If you have a couple of plants in the garden you are guaranteed to have a fairly bountiful summer harvest wherever you may be, even more so if you have a greenhouse. It also makes life easier if you have your own because if you want them open and easy to stuff, they need to be picked before the sun rises.

You can serve this recipe as a starter, either hot or at room temperature, as part of a buffet, or as an accompaniment to a rack of lamb or fillet of sea bass.

For 4

12 courgette flowers, as open as possible

1 onion, peeled and finely chopped

4 large garlic cloves, peeled and finely chopped

8 tbsp extra virgin olive oil

6 medium tomatoes, about 600g (1lb 5oz)

30g (1¼oz) dried breadcrumbs

salt and cayenne pepper

20 or so cherry tomatoes, halved

finely grated zest and juice of 1 lemon

1 small bunch fresh basil, leaves picked from the stalks, sliced

Preheat your oven to 190°C/375°F/Gas 5.

First sweat the onion and garlic in 2 tbsp of the olive oil for 5 minutes until soft but not coloured. Meanwhile core, roughly chop then purée the tomatoes. Add them to the onions and garlic and boil over a high heat until almost all of the liquid has gone. Add the breadcrumbs and 2 more tbsp of the olive oil. Season really well with salt and cayenne and leave to cool.

For the dressing, mix the halved cherry tomatoes with the zest and juice of the lemon, the basil and remaining olive oil. Season with plenty of salt and cayenne and set aside.

Stuff the courgette flowers with the tomato and onion mixture. Don't worry if they tear: just fill them and turn them upside down. Bake them in the preheated oven on an oiled tray for 5 minutes and serve with the tomato dressing.

BEIGNETS DE COURGETTES ET SES FLEURS
Courgette Fritters

Beignets *are as popular a starter as you get in Provence. Whether they're made with sardines or courgettes, the main thing is that the batter is light. The mixture of plain and potato flours here, and not too much mixing, achieves that.* Beignets *are usually served either alone or with lemon, but I much prefer a bowl of thick aïoli (see page 92).*

FOR 4
12 COURGETTE FLOWERS
2 LARGE COURGETTES, FINELY SLICED AT AN ANGLE
SALT
VEGETABLE OIL FOR DEEP-FRYING

BATTER
1 EGG YOLK
275ML (9½FL OZ) WATER
½ TSP SALT
100G (3½OZ) PLAIN FLOUR
100G (3½OZ) POTATO FLOUR
1 SMALL BUNCH FRESH BASIL

PREHEAT YOUR OVEN TO 180°C/350°F/GAS 4.
Remove the bases from the courgette flowers and open them out. Put the courgette slices with the flowers.

For the batter, mix the egg yolk with the water and salt, then add the flour, potato flour and basil with a wooden spoon. Don't stir too much; it's fine if you have a few pockets of flour.

Prepare an oven tray with plenty of kitchen paper and have a container of salt at the ready before you start frying. Heat your frying oil to 190°C/375°F.

Dip the flowers and courgettes in the batter and fry them in a single layer, in batches depending on the size of your fryer, for a couple of minutes each side. They should be light gold in colour. Lift them out with a spider, drain well, and put them on the tray with the kitchen paper in the oven. Season with salt and leave the oven door ajar while you continue. Serve piping hot.

Tarte Fine aux Tomates
Tomato Tart

I came across a tart like this one evening in a packed little restaurant in St Tropez. They made it with goat's cheese topped with dried tomatoes, but after a few tries I found it nicer to use fresh tomatoes so their juices flow out and then get sucked back up by the pastry. Don't worry if after half an hour the tart looks an absolute mess: it'll all dry out. The tomatoes will concentrate to an intensely flavoured, almost dry, crimson. You can eat the tart hot or cold and it's worth making for the aroma alone. I often serve this tart as part of a buffet, or sometimes I make individual ones and serve them with a sharply dressed salad and a Parmesan mayonnaise – simply add 150g (5½oz) freshly grated Parmesan to the aïoli recipe on page 92.

For 6
350G (12OZ) PUFF PASTRY

1.5KG (3LB 5OZ) TOMATOES, ALL AROUND THE SAME SIZE

150G (5½OZ) MASCARPONE CHEESE

50G (1¾OZ) PARMESAN, FRESHLY GRATED

1 BIGGISH BUNCH FRESH BASIL, LEAVES PICKED FROM THE STALKS, SLICED

SALT AND FRESHLY GROUND BLACK PEPPER

PREHEAT YOUR OVEN TO 200°C/400°F/GAS 6.

Roll the puff pastry to a circle slightly larger than 30cm (12in) in diameter. (If you don't have a ring this size, use a plate.) Put the pastry circle on a tray and let it rest in the fridge for 20 minutes or so while you prepare the tomatoes. Remove the cores from the tomatoes and slice them about 5mm thick. Keep all the slices together and put the ends in a separate pile.

Mix the mascarpone with the Parmesan and basil and season well. Spread the mascarpone across the centre of the pastry circle, leaving about 10cm (4in) at the edges. Layer the sliced tomatoes around the outside of the cheese, making a full circle. Continue towards the centre in ever-decreasing circles, overlapping the earlier circle each time. Tuck the tomato ends under each layer to prevent them caving in, then continue toward the centre. Put the last slice right in the middle.

Bake the tart in the preheated oven for 30 minutes, then turn the oven down to 150°C/300°F/Gas 2 and bake for a further 45 minutes. When cooked there should be almost no liquid left in the tomatoes, and the pastry base will be crisp.

GRATIN DE BLETTES
Swiss Chard Gratin

We're extremely fond of gratins in Provence, and with its crispy top and creamy centre this is one of the most loved. Blettes, *which are known either as Swiss chard or silver beet, are widely used and much easier to get hold of than spinach. The green variety is a pale, almost olive green and has fewer or smaller stalks, and the white has large white stalks and beautiful, white-veined, dark green leaves. The whole of the vegetable is used, but not always in the same dish, as the leaves cook a lot quicker than the stalks. The stalks are peeled lightly by just snapping them in half and pulling away the stringy bits. They are then sliced, blanched and sautéed with a little garlic, rosemary and parsley. You can add the leaves halfway through the cooking or do them as a separate dish, stewed slowly with plenty of onions, tomatoes and thyme. They're also quite nice blanched and tossed in a herby olive oil vinaigrette.*

FOR 6
1 LARGE HEAD OF SWISS CHARD, ABOUT 500G (1LB 2OZ), LEAVES AND RIBS SEPARATED
40G (1½OZ) BUTTER
30G (1¼OZ) PLAIN FLOUR
250ML (9FL OZ) MILK
150G (5½OZ) GRUYERE CHEESE, FRESHLY GRATED
100G (3½OZ) PROVENCAL BREADCRUMBS (SEE PAGE 31)
SALT AND FRESHLY GROUND BLACK PEPPER
FRESHLY GRATED NUTMEG

PREHEAT YOUR OVEN TO 180°C/350°F/GAS 4.
Melt the butter in a small saucepan, turn off the heat and add the flour. Stir to remove any lumps, then stir in the milk. Put back on the heat and bring to the boil gently, stirring all the time. Boil for a minute then add 100g of Gruyère and keep stirring until it has melted. Remove from the heat.

Chop the Swiss chard ribs into 1cm (½in) slices and boil them in plenty of salted water. Slice the leaves and add these when the ribs are almost tender. Boil for a further 2 minutes. Strain and dry well, then mix with the cheese sauce and spoon into a gratin dish. Sprinkle with the breadcrumbs and remaining cheese, and bake in the preheated oven for about 20 minutes until the top is golden and bubbling.

PROVENCAL BREADCRUMBS

These are a must! Keep your old bits of bread, dry them in a low oven and store them in an airtight container ready to make these or plain crumbs. You can make them in reasonably large quantities and freeze them in bags, just taking out a handful when you need them. They can be used with the lamb on page 108, on top of grilled aubergines or peppers, baked with a little fresh or salt cod or sprinkled with a little good parmesan over grilled tomatoes. I've even used them mixed with gruyère, on top of macaroni cheese. Close your eyes and inhale when you make them and you will have an instant hit of Provence no matter where you are.

MAKES APPROX 150G (5½OZ)

1 SMALL BUNCH OF FLAT LEAF PARSLEY, LEAVES PICKED FROM THE STALKS

4 GOOD SIZE SPRIGS OF SAVORY, THYME, OR ROSEMARY,
   LEAVES PICKED FROM THE STALKS

2 CLOVES OF GARLIC, PEELED AND ROUGHLY CHOPPED

100G (3½OZ) DRIED BREAD

2TBS EXTRA VIRGIN OLIVE OIL

SALT AND FRESHLY GROUND BLACK PEPPER

METHOD

Blend the parsley, savory and garlic until fine. Crush the dried bread a little with your hands; add it to the herb mixture and using the pulse button blend to a coarse texture. Add the olive oil and season well. Keep airtight in the freezer until you need them.

BETTERAVE ROTIE AU FROMAGE DE CHEVRE
Roasted Beetroot with Fresh Goat's Cheese

To be able to buy pre-cooked beetroot in our local Provençal markets has been a wonderful discovery. I can waive the hour or so that's needed to boil or bake a big beetroot, and peel and use them straightaway, making them a much more practical proposition for everyday eating. They are at their best when just picked from July to September. I've found to my great delight that slicing and roasting them has won over many friends who said they'd always disliked beets but would just try one to keep me happy. When roasted and caramelised, almost dry around the outside and melting in the middle, the flavour marries perfectly with creamy fresh goat's cheese and spicy rocket.

FOR 6
2 LARGE COOKED BEETROOT, ABOUT 800G (1LB 12OZ)
SALT AND FRESHLY GROUND BLACK PEPPER
4 TBSP GROUNDNUT OIL
200G (7OZ) FRESH GOAT'S CHEESE (BISCARON, ST MAURE, ANYTHING CREAMY)
1 BUNCH ROCKET
100G (3½OZ) SEMI-DRIED TOMATOES
100ML (3½FL OZ) OLIVE OIL
2 TBSP BALSAMIC VINEGAR

PREHEAT YOUR OVEN TO 190°C/375°F/GAS 5.
Cut each beetroot in half, then each half into six wedges. Lay these flat on a tray just large enough to hold them, season them well and pour over the oil. Roast the beetroot for 15 minutes each side.

You can either serve them straightaway or at room temperature. In either case, chop the goat's cheese into chunks and slice the rocket. Scatter these and the whole semi-dried tomatoes over the top of the beetroot wedges. Drizzle with the olive oil and vinegar, grind over plenty of pepper, and serve.

BANON ROTI, TOMATES CERISES
Roast Banon Cheese with Cherry Tomatoes

I happened on this combination when I had a seemingly endless supply of cherry tomatoes from the garden and was eating them this way or that with every meal. You could, I suppose, use large tomatoes, but it was the intensely sweet flavour of the little ones combined with the piquancy of the cheese and the salty ham that really did it for me. Banon, the cheese wrapped in chestnut leaves from northern Provence, is my cheese of choice, but failing that you could use a strong goat's cheese that slices easily, such as St Maure. You can toast the baguette but I prefer not to, just allowing it to crisp a little on top and letting the soggy bottom soak up the rich, sweet juice from the tomatoes.

FOR 4
2 WHOLE BANON CHEESES, REMOVED FROM THEIR LEAVES
200G (7OZ) VERY RIPE CHERRY TOMATOES
SALT AND FRESHLY GROUND BLACK PEPPER
50ML (2FL OZ) OLIVE OIL
2 THICK SLICES CURED HAM, CUT INTO MATCHSTICKS
4 SLICES BAGUETTE, CUT AT AN ANGLE

PREHEAT YOUR GRILL TO ITS HIGHEST SETTING.
Halve the cheeses horizontally through the middle. Put the cherry tomatoes in a pan and add a little salt and half of the olive oil. Cook over a medium heat for about 10 minutes until the tomatoes have begun to burst and liquefy. Add the ham matchsticks, and keep warm.

While the tomatoes are cooking, put the cheese on top of the baguette slices, drizzle with the remaining olive oil and season well with salt and pepper. Grill for about 5 minutes, and serve on top of the tomatoes.

Au Bord de la Mer

The Provençaux have a passion for their fruit of the sea that borders on obsession.
If you get caught up in the excitement of a fish market (our closest is St Tropez), hear
the shouting and bartering, and put up with the occasional shove in the back, you
experience how much they want – and will have, thank you very much – their
seafood. Shimmering piles of red mullet, *daurade*, sea bass, anchovies and sardines
diminish during the early morning sales at an astonishing speed. The marble and
concrete hall in which the market is held is not that large, but seems so in summer
with such a variety on display – not only of fish but also St Tropez glamour and
tourists from all over the world.

It's a real crush. If you don't get there early, as the crowds swell it is difficult to get fish
or even to move. Turning around is impossible: you have to go outside and come back
in again from the other direction. Each stallholder is shouting, meeting your eyes if
they can, and doing everything possible to grab your attention. They'll insist theirs are
the best fish, the freshest wild sea bass, the smoothest squid, the fattest *gambas* and
heaviest, juice-filled, most sublime oysters and *violets* (knobbly rock-encrusting creatures
also known as sea figs). Each fishmonger is so, so proud and truly enthusiastic. They are
real artisans and genuinely delighted when you choose something from their stall.
They're also quite happy to charge you through the nose, smiling as they do so.

Most fish dishes in Provence are very simply cooked. Sea bass or the many different
sorts of sea bream will be stuffed full of fennel and grilled over charcoal and vine
clippings, or, as I prefer, baked with lots of olive oil, garlic and orange peel. Because of
this simplicity, as with any dish where the ingredients are left to speak for themselves,
the fish need to be as sparklingly fresh as possible, carefully selected and lovingly
cooked.

The magical thing about an open fish market is that first you find the fish, or, staring
out from his bed of ice, the bright-eyed devil finds you. Then you decide what you are
going to have with it. While you're buying some bread for an aperitif, or a few
peaches, the fishmonger is deftly scaling, gutting and lovingly packaging your choice.

I often stop at the sardines. Perfectly fresh, shiny and silver-blue, firm to the touch
and bright of eye, they're irresistible. They are also invariably the best value catch
and, once scaled, easy to work with. Grilled, fried or baked whole with a smattering

of salt, a good squeeze of lemon and some olive oil, they make a sort of old-fashioned feast. Greedy fingers pick the flesh from the bones as piles of little skeletons build up at the side of each plate. This is a wonderful way to eat them, but you don't need a full-blown recipe for that. In the sardine recipes in this chapter they are carefully boned, stuffed with Swiss chard and pine nuts and baked with lemon, or simply grilled and served with tomato compote, olives and lemon.

Of all the crustaceans on offer, very few come from the Mediterranean. One type that does, and that I now use whenever I can, is the selection of prawn or *gamba*, going from the fairly small, each about 6cm (2½in), up to the enormous *camarones* (one of which I bought and devoured alone was a mite over 600g – 1lb 5oz – or the size of an average lobster). Their flesh is sweeter and less prone to becoming like cotton wool than lobster or langoustines. They can be cooked in all manner of wonderful ways: grilled in their shells, oozing with herb or tomato butter; shelled and pan-fried until golden, then doused with olive oil and pepper; steamed and served warm to be lovingly peeled from their shells and dipped into thick, garlicky aïoli. (This is undoubtedly one of the best things to eat in the early stages of romance, being not only naturally sexy, but also suggestive.) If I strip the shells before cooking, I always keep them. As they are much thinner than the shells of lobster, they can be very quickly cooked, releasing their flavour completely in about 10 minutes to make incredibly fragrant and intense stocks and bisques.

There are also the highly regarded spider crabs (I have only ever seen one or two at a time), the *langoustes* and *cigales de mer* (a flat, lobster-like crustacean). All three are delicious and regarded as luxuries. They are now extremely rare, fetching massively high prices, which is not too much of a problem for St Tropéziens but still astonishing when you do the maths. The last time I saw a *cigale de mer* I got gazumped while thinking about the £30 price tag. I turned around, having decided to buy it, as it was loaded, its tail flapping, into the basket of a young man with a crew cut and a rich boss waiting in his gin palace. I really should know by now just to push, shove and grab when I see something I like.

After the hustle and bustle of the morning, things start to quieten down in the market around midday. The bars on the port are crowded, waiters are hastily chalking their specialities of *Daurade*, *Loup* and *Chapon* on their restaurant blackboards, and grills are being lit on patios all down the coast. After one o'clock only the odd scale and pile of melting ice would tell you that that the fish market had been there at all. The halls are hosed down and all the fisher folk have gone for lunch or a game of boules.

SARDINES GRILLEES, SAUCE VIERGE
Grilled Sardines with Tomatoes

Both the sauce vierge *and the tomato compote are high on the list of wonderful preparations that accompany and enhance almost anything. Try both or either with lamb cutlets, grilled aubergines, peppers and mozzarella, or even with just a thick slice of crisp, garlicky, olive-oil-rich grilled bread.*

Once you've tried boning the sardines, you'll be surprised at how simple it is and, as you get the hang of it, how very satisfying as well.

FOR 4
20 SARDINES
1 RECIPE *COMPOTE DE TOMATES* (SEE PAGE 165)
SALT AND CAYENNE PEPPER

SAUCE VIERGE
100ML (3½FL OZ) EXTRA VIRGIN OLIVE OIL
FINELY GRATED ZEST AND JUICE OF 1 LEMON
20 CHERRY TOMATOES, HALVED
12 BLACK OLIVES, STONED AND HALVED
SMALL BUNCH OF FRESH BASIL, LEAVES PICKED FROM THE STALKS, SLICED

PREHEAT YOUR GRILL TO ITS HIGHEST SETTING.
Very gently scrape the scales from the sardines with the back of a knife. Give the fish a good rinse, then cut off the heads, slit the bellies and remove the innards. Press your thumb along the inside of the central bone then open the sardines outwards with the thumb and forefinger of your other hand and remove the bone. Give them another quick rinse then store them flat, skin side up in the fridge until you need them.

Make the tomato compote and keep warm. Mix the ingredients for the *sauce vierge* together, season well and set aside.

Finally, put the sardines skin side up flat on a tray that will fit under your grill, brush them with some of the oil from the *sauce vierge* and season with salt and cayenne. Grill for 5 minutes until the sardines are soft and the skin is just starting to blister.

Serve with the warmed tomato compote and the *sauce vierge*.

SARDINES FARCIS AUX BLETTES
Sardines with Swiss Chard

I first encountered this combination at a tiny restaurant in Cogolin. It has only six tables and is run by a charming husband and wife, with a hard-working dishwasher the only member of staff. There are three or four choices for each course, always totally seasonal, perfectly seasoned and delicious, and these are changed daily according to the movement of the markets. This dish is a regular feature.

FOR 4
12 VERY FRESH SARDINES

1 SMALL HEAD SWISS CHARD, ABOUT 250G (9OZ)

6 GARLIC CLOVES, PEELED AND FINELY CHOPPED

1 SMALL ONION, PEELED AND FINELY CHOPPED

2 LARGE SPRIGS FRESH THYME, LEAVES PICKED FROM THE STALKS

120ML (4FL OZ) OLIVE OIL

50G (1¾OZ) COARSE BREADCRUMBS

50G (1¾OZ) PINE NUTS

SALT AND FRESHLY GROUND BLACK PEPPER

VEGETABLE OIL FOR GREASING

2 LEMONS

PREHEAT YOUR OVEN TO 200°C/400°F/GAS 6.

Prepare the sardines as on page 41, then pop them in the fridge until you need them. Separate the stalks and leaves of the Swiss chard, then dice the stalks finely or chop them in the food processor. Sweat the diced stalks along with the garlic, chopped onion and thyme for 5 minutes in half the olive oil until they soften, but don't let them colour. While this is going on, slice the Swiss chard leaves finely. Add them to the pan, and cook over a high heat, stirring all the time for about 5 minutes until the vegetables are totally soft. Remove from the heat, add the breadcrumbs and pine nuts, season well and set aside.

Lay the sardines flat on a greased baking tray, skin side down. Put a spoonful of the chard mixture on the non-tail end of each, then fold the tail back over. (If you have any mixture left, you can heat it, and serve it on the side.) Season the sardines well and squeeze over the juice of 1 lemon. Bake for about 5 minutes in the preheated oven. While they are cooking mix the juice of the second lemon with the remaining olive oil, season well then spoon over and around the sardines.

Daurade Grillee au Pistou de Coquillage
Grilled Sea Bream with a 'Pistou' of Shellfish

I used marbré, *the very beautiful marbled sea bream, for the photo, but any type of sea bream would be fine. The silver-blue* daurade royale, *the* daurade rose *known in Italy as* bocca d'oro *for its golden mouth, and the pink-gold* pagre *are often stuffed with fennel and grilled whole or cooked in crusts of sea salt. This mixture is a type of* soupe au pistou *with shellfish added. The pistou mixture can be cooked a few hours in advance up to the point of adding the shellfish. Should you find fresh beans difficult to obtain, just omit them.*

For 4

4 LARGE FILLETS SEA BREAM, EACH 150G (5½ OZ) PLUS
A LITTLE EXTRA VIRGIN OLIVE OIL FOR GRILLING
SALT AND FRESHLY GROUND BLACK PEPPER

Pistou of shellfish

1 LARGE RED PEPPER, SEEDED AND CUT INTO LARGE DICE
50ML (2FL OZ) EXTRA VIRGIN OLIVE OIL
1 SMALL WHITE ONION, PEELED AND ROUGHLY CHOPPED
2 GARLIC CLOVES, PEELED AND CUT INTO LARGE DICE
500G (1LB 2OZ) FRESH WHITE HARICOT BEANS, 250G (9OZ) SHELLED WEIGHT
1 LARGE COURGETTE, CUT INTO LARGE DICE
24 CLAMS, WELL RINSED
24 MUSSELS, DE-BEARDED AND RINSED
3 ROMA TOMATOES, SEEDED AND CHOPPED
1 SMALL BUNCH FRESH BASIL, LEAVES PICKED FROM THE STALKS, CHOPPED

PREHEAT YOUR GRILL TO ITS HIGHEST SETTING.
Sweat the diced red pepper in the oil for 5 minutes, then add the onion and garlic and sweat for 5 minutes more. Add the beans and just enough water to cover, then simmer for 25 minutes until the beans are soft and the liquid has all but gone. Transfer the mixture to a large shallow pan with a tight-fitting lid and add the courgette, clams and mussels. Cover and cook quickly for about 5 minutes until the shellfish open (discard any that don't).

While the shellfish are cooking, lay the fillets of bream on a tray, brush them with olive oil, season well and grill for 6-8 minutes. Mix the chopped tomato and basil with the shellfish mixture and serve with the bream.

GIGOT DE LOTTE
Baked Monkfish

Gigot *usually refers to a leg of lamb. This is a little Provençal twist, as the garlic-studded tapering tail end of the monkfish resembles a* gigot.

FOR 4

1 LARGE PIECE MONKFISH, ABOUT 1KG (2LB 4OZ)
8 SMALL ARTICHOKES, TRIMMED
16 SMALL POTATOES, SCRUBBED
12 SHALLOTS, PEELED
SALT AND FRESHLY GROUND BLACK PEPPER
JUICE OF 2 LEMONS
100ML (3½FL OZ) OLIVE OIL
4 GARLIC CLOVES, PEELED
1 SMALL BUNCH FRESH THYME, LEAVES PICKED FROM THE STALKS
150ML (5FL OZ) DRY WHITE WINE
1 SMALL DRIED CHILLI
4 STRIPS DRIED ORANGE ZEST (SEE PAGE 173)
1 BUNCH FRESH FLAT-LEAF PARSLEY, LEAVES PICKED FROM THE STALKS, SLICED

PREHEAT YOUR OVEN TO 190°C/375°F/GAS 5.
Boil the artichokes, potatoes and shallots in plenty of salted water with the juice of one of the lemons for 20 minutes until almost cooked. Strain them, toss with a third of the olive oil, salt and pepper, then put them in the bottom of an ovenproof dish.

Make a dozen or so little incisions in the monkfish. Slice the garlic into slivers and push them into the holes. Put the monkfish into the dish with the artichokes, potatoes and shallots, pour over a little more olive oil and sprinkle with some of the thyme, salt and pepper. Roast for 35 minutes, then check with a skewer at the thickest part of the fish. If the tip comes out warm, remove the monkfish from the dish. Keep it warm, and put the vegetables back in the oven for 5-10 minutes until well browned.

Pick the garlic out of the fish, chop it and mix with the white wine, juice of the second lemon, dried chilli and orange zest. Reduce all of this by half. Stir in the remaining olive oil and thyme and the flat-leaf parsley, and spoon over the monkfish. To serve, slice both fillets of monkfish away from the bone and cut each in half in turn. Serve with the vegetables.

ROUGET A LA TAPENADE
Red Mullet with Tapenade

Red mullet is known as the woodcock of the sea because, as with the bird, it is traditionally cooked whole, insides and all. A thick sauce is then made using the latter as a base. It's rarely done this way now, but red mullet is still one of the most popular and certainly most strongly flavoured of Mediterranean fish, which is why I've partnered it with the salty strength of tapenade.

FOR 4
8 LARGE FILLETS OF RED MULLET
2 MEDIUM AUBERGINES
OLIVE OIL
JUICE OF 2 LEMONS
1 MILD CHILLI, SEEDED AND FINELY CHOPPED
2 GARLIC CLOVES, PEELED AND FINELY CHOPPED
SALT AND CAYENNE PEPPER
250G (9OZ) *CONFIT DE TOMATES* (SEE PAGE 166)
5 SPRIGS FRESH THYME, LEAVES PICKED FROM THE STALKS
16 BLACK OLIVES, STONED AND CHOPPED
150G (5½OZ) RECIPE *TAPENADE* (SEE PAGE 168)

PREHEAT YOUR GRILL TO HIGH.
Peel the aubergines and cut them into French-fry-sized sticks. Put them in a pan with 100ml (3½fl oz) of the olive oil, the juice of one of the lemons, the chilli and garlic. Cook over a moderate heat for about 15 minutes without colouring until they are soft and creamy. Season with salt and cayenne.

In the meantime mix 50ml (2fl oz) of olive oil with the juice of the second lemon, the *confit* tomatoes, thyme and olives. Warm lightly and season well with salt and cayenne.

Brush the red mullet fillets with oil, season them lightly and grill for 5 minutes, skin side up. Spread some tapenade on every second fillet and serve with the aubergine and tomato and olive dressing.

Moules Grillees au Basilic
Grilled Mussels with Basil

If you prefer them with butter don't deny yourself (I rarely do), but using a good olive oil makes a lovely change. The rich, aromatic cooking juices can be used later for braising potatoes or, to make more of a meal of things, you could make some extra pistou *and mix it with the juices for a broth to serve either just before or after the mussels.*

For 4

4 dozen large mussels
1 bunch fresh basil, leaves picked from the stalks,
    blanched for 30 seconds and refreshed
4 fat garlic cloves, peeled
50-80ml (2-3fl oz) olive oil, as good as the budget will allow
2 large tomatoes, seeded and finely chopped
finely grated zest and juice of 1 lemon
50g (1¾oz) dried breadcrumbs
freshly ground black pepper

Preheat your grill to its highest setting.
De-beard and wash your mussels, throwing away any that are cracked or that are open and don't close when you give them a little tap. Get a big, preferably shallow pan with a tight-fitting lid and put the mussels in. Pour over a little water, put the lid on top and make sure it fits snugly before boiling the mussels over your highest heat, just giving them the odd shake, for a few minutes. You want your mussels only just open as you will be cooking them a second time. Remove and discard any that don't open at all, and strain the liquid to use in one of the ways I've suggested above.

Let the mussels cool until you can handle them, then prise off the top shells. Lay the bottom shells with the mussels flat on a tray that will fit under your grill.

Purée the basil and garlic with the olive oil in your food processor to a thick paste, then add the tomatoes, lemon zest and juice, breadcrumbs and some pepper. Smear this over the top of the mussels and grill them until they are sizzling and crispy around the edges.

Moules au Safran
Mussels with Saffron

A big bowl of mussels – spanking fresh, steaming and smacking of the sea – is the quickest way of having a wonderful meal. Every time I get anywhere near a raw one I have a scary trip down memory lane, not to the first time I ate a great bowlful but to my early days in France when working in Burgundy. There I was stuck in the fish-preparation area for days at a time, scraping and scrubbing the shells to remove even the tiniest of barnacles. I would then soak them in salt, rinse them endlessly and pass them to the head fish guy. He would, minutes later, pass them back cooked and my then very raw fingers would remove and throw away the thousands of shells that I had earlier cleaned. At the end of one of these days (and almost my tether), I asked the chef why he bothered wasting time in this way. I received the standard response relating to the ignorance of those born outside of France, and so I had to keep on scraping until relief came (or so I thought) about a month later, in the form of the vegetable section.

For 4
2kg (4lb 8oz) mussels
150ml (5fl oz) dry white wine
100ml (3½fl oz) extra virgin olive oil
4 garlic cloves, peeled and finely chopped
large pinch of saffron strands
1 small dried chilli, finely crumbled
4 large slices of bread, toasted

First of all de-beard the mussels by pulling the hairy part towards the fat end of the shells then out. If there are any barnacles, remove them. If there are any open, give them a good tap and if they don't close of their own accord throw them away. Rinse them well and store beneath a wet tea-towel until you need them.

In a large shallow pan, boil the white wine together with the olive oil, garlic, saffron and chilli for a few minutes until they begin to emulsify. Add the mussels, cover the pan and cook for about 5 minutes over as high a heat as possible, stirring the mussels once or twice so that they open evenly (discard any that don't). Serve over the top of the toasted bread.

Fricassee de Gambas, Moules et Coques
Fricassee of Prawns, Mussels and Cockles

This is a mixture of all that's good about cooking simply in the Provençal way. All you're really doing is opening the shellfish and giving them a little more punch with the tiger prawn stock. Each flavour stands out individually, but they all merge into a feast for the nose and palate.

For 4

20 raw tiger prawns in their shells
1 tbsp tomato concentrate
4 dozen mussels
4 dozen small clams
1 onion, peeled and finely sliced
2 small carrots, peeled and finely sliced
1 medium leek, washed and sliced
4 tbsp olive oil
1 small bunch fresh basil, leaves picked from the stalks, finely chopped

Remove the heads and shells from the tiger prawns, keeping the prawns to one side. Put the heads and shells in a pot with the tomato concentrate, just cover with water and bring to the boil. Simmer for 15 minutes, then strain and reduce by half. Reserve.

De-beard all of the mussels and rinse them and the clams very well. If any are slightly open, tap them lightly and if they don't close, discard them.

In a large shallow pan with a tight-fitting lid sweat the onion, carrot and leek in the olive oil for 10 minutes, without colouring, until totally soft. Pour the tiger prawn stock over the vegetables and bring to the boil. Add the prawns, mussels and cockles, and boil until all of the mussels and clams open (discard any that don't), about 5 minutes. Toss with the basil and serve.

SOUPE DE GAMBAS AUX CONFIT DE TOMATES
Tiger Prawn Soup with Confit Tomatoes

One of the wonderful by-products of buying bread daily are recipes like this, developed over time to use up the leftovers. This is a type of gazpacho enriched with the gamba stock. Sweet, plump gambas, or tiger prawns, are the simplest of crustaceans to use: they peel like a dream, the shells break up easily and produce the most fragrant of all bisques. I serve this soup cold but if you prefer it hot you could just leave out the cucumber and the bread. You can make it a day or so before you serve it.

FOR 4
12 RAW TIGER PRAWNS IN THEIR SHELLS
3 TBSP VEGETABLE OIL

2 TSP TOMATO CONCENTRATE
1 LARGE RED PEPPER, SEEDED AND ROUGHLY CHOPPED
¼ ENGLISH CUCUMBER, ROUGHLY CHOPPED
2 LARGE, VERY RIPE ROMA TOMATOES
2 GARLIC CLOVES, PEELED
50G (1¾OZ) BREAD, SOAKED IN 100ML (3½FL OZ) OLIVE OIL
50ML (2FL OZ) WATER
SALT AND CAYENNE PEPPER
PINCH OF CASTER SUGAR (OPTIONAL)

TO SERVE
250G (9OZ) *CONFIT DE TOMATES* (SEE PAGE 166), USING CHERRY TOMATOES
1 TBSP *PISTOU* (SEE PAGE 170)

Twist off the heads of the tiger prawns, then remove the shells starting from the underside of the prawns, leaving just the last piece of shell with the tail on. Keep all the heads and shells for the sauce. Next, slit the prawns down their backs, not cutting through them completely, and remove the intestine. Set aside.

Sauté the tiger prawn shells for a minute or so in half the oil until the shells begin to change colour, then add the tomato concentrate. Sauté for a further minute until the tomato concentrate starts to darken, then cover the prawns with water. Bring to the boil and skim, then cook over a fairly high heat for 10 minutes. Purée the shells with the liquid in a food processor and strain through a fine sieve. Set aside.

Purée the red pepper, cucumber, tomatoes, garlic, the olive-oil-soaked bread and the water in a blender together with the stock made from the tiger prawn shells. Season well with salt and cayenne. The soup is great if there is a little bite to it. Add a pinch of sugar if necessary.

Fry the tiger prawns in the remaining oil for 3-4 minutes until they are bright pink and no longer transparent. Serve the soup in deep plates, topped with the prawns and the *confit* tomatoes. Drizzle over the *pistou* and serve.

ON THE PRAWN SHELLS
If you are using tiger prawns for anything without the shells, keep the latter, freeze them and bring them out when you have enough to make either this recipe or a bisque on its own.

BOUILLABAISSE AND OTHER STORIES

This chapter is a celebration of Provence's best-known dishes, among them *salade Niçoise*, *pissaladière*, and the tomato- and orange-scented *daube de boeuf*. But the most legendary of them all is the famous bouillabaisse.

Just a mention of bouillabaisse stirs up a powerful image for anyone who loves to eat. Richly scented, bright with saffron and the orange-red of its rockfish, everything about a good one conjures up visions of a Provençal feast. The name, evocative as it now may be, has more practical origins, thought to come from the Provençal *boui* (to boil) and *baisser* (to lower). With a little imagination this could be the very short, original recipe, 'Boil your broth, add your fish and lower the heat.' Which is exactly how Marseillais fishermen would make it: on the beach over a driftwood fire, where the remains of their catch too small, spiny or ugly to sell were cooked in salt water and olive oil. A fish would have earlier been swapped for some tomatoes and fennel for flavour, and thick chunks of bread served as both plates and second course.

Today bouillabaisse is a dish which all over Provence is the root cause of more arguments than any other. These feisty discussions are often better than the soup itself. I love to listen, watch and only join in as cheekily as possible when things show signs of slowing down. A foreigner participating at all gets the eyes bulging and the corks popping. More so if I mention my more recent refinements. Yes, I fillet the fish first! Of course I cook it in the oven! *Gambas*? As many as possible! Given a chance I describe my first bouillabaisse.

In Marseille, nineteen years old, brimming with excitement, I went out early to watch the fishermen bring in their catch and their wives arrange it on their shaded seaweed- and ice-filled tables. Sparkling *daurade rose* and *loup de mer* for grilling lay alongside huge *chapons* for stuffing, sardines for marinades and tiny rockfish for *la soupe*. Each fisherman seemed to have unearthed a treasure too. On one table was a huge spider crab with its legs roped; on another a flat tank-like *cigale de mer* and a basket of wrinkled *violets*, a mollusc scented more strongly of the sea than any oyster. On yet another, a dead looking octopus which wrapped itself around my arm and gave rise to an almighty cackle from the surrounding fishwives while scaring me senseless and momentarily putting me off the idea of prodding everything, as I thought was so expected at any French market. Each sale is a social event: first the recipe is discussed and the relative merits of each fish are compared (somewhat cagily in case a better choice is spotted at a rival's table). The fish is scaled and gutted, sometimes filleted, and the carcasses are kept for soup or stock, if not thrown to the seagulls that lurk hopefully all around. The larger fish to be cooked whole are stuffed full of dried wild fennel stalks that are in boxes underneath each table.

My booking at the restaurant where I was sent by the tourist office (first mistake) was at 1 pm. I went back to the youth hostel and changed carefully into my good trousers and shirt which I'd put under my mattress to press the night before. I ordered a *pastis* and looked at the different options for my bouillabaisse while counting my money under my napkin. I had just enough, and asked for a half lobster with my bouillabaisse. I very carefully went through what I wanted with the waiter and settled into my aperitif and olives.

The bouillabaisse arrived with the sort of proud panache that only the French can muster. It also arrived with half a *langouste* in place of half a *homard* sitting on top. A *langouste*, being a rock lobster, is the traditional crustacean in a bouillabaisse, but I didn't care I wanted my claw. I pointed this out – he of course pointed out that I was wrong, and not French, let alone Marseillais, and therefore ignorant. Neither wanting nor really having the language to be able to get into a great discussion about it all I said OK and made a saddened start to my bouillabaisse. The fish itself was stringy and cold. The *langouste* had the texture of cotton wool. The soup was so overpoweringly fishy that after a few spoonfuls I was beaten. I paid my bill, weathered the sneer of the waiter and walked back along the port where the fishermen's wives were long finished.

The next bouillabaisse I ate was a couple of years later. At the end of a season cooking in the Alps, I caught a lift to the south of France with a few friends, one of whom, Laurent, had a father with a restaurant in Gassin. This bouillabaisse was the real thing, not just in the eating but in the anticipation. Laurent's father showed us all of the fish early in the morning, took me through the different types – the *chapons, rascasses, vives*, congers, the multi-coloured *wrasse* and lively little crabs known as *étrilles*. There was a big box of the tiny versions of all these fish destined for the *soupe de poisson*, a mixture so colourful it was like looking through a kaleidoscope.

The fish were picked free of twigs but not seaweed and just rinsed, not cleaned. We helped him scale and empty the larger fish, instructed to be careful and keep the intensely flavoured livers for the *rouille*. He then cut off all the heads, slicing at an angle just behind the gills to get the maximum of flesh at the thickest part of the fish.

(I remembered Laurent once ridiculing another of the chefs in the Alps, completely disgusted because he had put carrots in a 'so-called' bouillabaisse. Seeing the care with which this one evolved, I began to understand the importance.)

The *soupe de poisson* went on to cook and we were given a basket of crudités, *anchoïade*, and some young red wine to whet our appetites while it cooked. We dipped young spring onions and finely sliced, lemon-rubbed baby artichokes, and played boules in the courtyard while the soup cooked inside. Laurent's dad started a wood fire next to the restaurant over which he hung a blackened cauldron. He poured in the rich fennel- and orange-scented soup, sprinkled over a small amount of saffron – 'Not too much, guys, or it'll taste like medicine' – and put the soup on to cook. He enquired after our game, watched a few throws and had a laugh at my amateurish efforts, then went back to his kitchen to get the fish. He filled the pot with the firmer fleshed fish in the bottom over the crabs then layered up the other fish and potatoes.

An hour or so later we went over to the terrace, which overlooks first vines and then the sea. We opened another few bottles of the young red, and Papa arrived with the bouillabaisse. The fish and crabs had been joined by small but plump mussels and were laid out in an enormous, hollowed piece of cork. The soup had been thickened with *rouille* and was ladled, steaming, from a huge tureen. There were croûtons and more *rouille* in a few sandy mortars. The next hour was not wasted on talk. Eyes and mouth went from fish to soup, and a sip of wine preceded a lingering glance at the sea. My three French friends later marvelled at my capacity, having finished long before I did. I explained that I'd had a memory to erase before I started anew, and we returned to the courtyard for another game of boules. The following is more or less the same recipe.

BOUILLABAISSE

The tiny fish used for the soup – known as soupe *or* soupe de poisson – *are smaller versions of the* rascasses, *weavers and John Dories used in the bouillabaisse itself.*

FOR 8

1 KG (2LB 4OZ) MONKFISH
8 *RASCASSES*
6 WEAVER FISH
2 JOHN DORIES
3 *WRASSES*

MARINADE

1 BOUQUET OF WILD FENNEL, CHOPPED
$\frac{1}{2}$ TSP POWDERED SAFFRON
4 GARLIC CLOVES, PEELED AND ROUGHLY CHOPPED
8 TBSP OLIVE OIL

FISH SOUP

2 LARGE ONIONS, PEELED AND SLICED
1 HEAD OF GARLIC, PEELED AND COARSELY CHOPPED
1 LARGE FENNEL BULB, SLICED
5 TBSP OLIVE OIL
3 TOMATOES, QUARTERED
1KG (2LB 4OZ) *SOUPE* (TINY WHOLE UNGUTTED ROCK FISH)
500G (1LB 2OZ) CONGER EEL, CUT INTO SMALL PIECES
10 SMALL, LIVE CRABS (*FAVOUILLES* OR *ETRILLES*)

ROUILLE

2 *RASCASSE* LIVERS, POACHED IN A LITTLE HOT FISH SOUP FOR 1 MINUTE
3 GARLIC CLOVES, PEELED
1 LARGE EGG YOLK
LARGE PINCH OF SALT
LARGE PINCH OF CAYENNE PEPPER
250G (9OZ) FRESH BREADCRUMBS
$\frac{1}{2}$ TSP SAFFRON THREADS, DISSOLVED IN 4 TBSP HOT FISH SOUP
400ML (14FL OZ) OLIVE OIL, AT ROOM TEMPERATURE

To finish

8 MEDIUM NEW POTATOES, PEELED AND SLICED 2CM (¾IN) THICK
1 LARGE ONION, PEELED AND SLICED AS FINELY AS POSSIBLE
3 ROMA TOMATOES, SEEDED
5 GARLIC CLOVES, PEELED AND FINELY CHOPPED
BOUQUET OF FENNEL STALKS
½ TSP SAFFRON THREADS
1KG (2LB 4OZ) MUSSELS, DE-BEARDED AND WELL RINSED
CROUTONS MADE FROM A LARGE BAGUETTE

Scale, gut and rinse the fish and spread them out on a tray. Sprinkle over the fennel, saffron, garlic and olive oil. Turn the fish a few times with your hands to make sure that they are well coated with oil and that the other ingredients are evenly distributed. Leave to marinate while you prepare the soup and the *rouille.*

For the fish soup, sweat the onion, garlic and fennel bulb in the olive oil until softened and translucent but not coloured. Add the tomatoes, fish and conger eel. Raise the heat and stir for about 5 minutes until the fish begins to break up. Pour over enough water to cover, bring to the boil and add the crabs. Bring back to the boil for 25 minutes, topping up with water if necessary. Pour the soup through a colander bit by bit, bashing the crabs and fish with a pestle then pressing down well to extract the maximum of liquid and flavour. Discard each pile of debris before doing the next lot. When you have done it all, strain the liquid through a fine sieve and set aside.

For the *rouille*, pound the *rascasse* livers and garlic to a smooth paste in a mortar. Add the egg yolk, a little salt, a good pinch of cayenne, the breadcrumbs and saffron mixture. Mash to a thick paste then add the olive oil very slowly as for a mayonnaise.

To finish and serve, reheat the fish soup, add the potato, onion, tomato, garlic, fennel and saffron, and return to the boil. Boil for 5 minutes and add the monkfish. Simmer for 5 minutes, then add the other fish and simmer for 15 minutes. Add the mussels and boil for 5 minutes until they all open (discard any that remain closed).With a large wire spider, lift the fish, mussels and vegetables on to a large heated serving dish (cork if you have it). Ladle some of the broth into a large heated soup tureen, leaving some in the pot for a second serving. You can then serve all at once to be passed around, or you can serve the soup first with the croûtons and *rouille* and keep the fish, vegetables and mussels warm to serve afterwards with a little of the soup thickened with *rouille.*

LE BAOU D'INFER BOUILLABAISSE
Our Bouillabaisse

As many versions as I have eaten, I have tried to cook more. This is a much refined version that has proved the simplest to eat and serve and the most adaptable to the different types of fish available in different countries. We started serving a 'true' bouillabaisse, but some of the guests, a little less keen, were defeated after 10 minutes or so of politely grimacing through little bones which they picked from their teeth. I was of course greedily sucking at every carcass, licking my fingers between each attack, but a single glance upward told me that work was needed to make the bouillabaisse a success. I then started to fillet the fish and make the broth similar to the recipe that I have laid out here. The broth was then strained and I poached the fish in a series of pans depending on its type before being lifted out on to trays and portioned. Lifting out fish fillets that cook through in a flash is somewhere between walking on a tightrope and eggshells, so quickly do they break up. I ended doing as I suggest here, baking the marinated fish fillets in stock in their portions, which makes for great ease of serving. If you want to serve the fish after the soup, you can easily put it in a big serving dish or in individual portions as you prefer; it can happily go into the oven as you take out the soup. From the pleasure point of view, though, I most enjoy serving it all at once.

If you can't get all of the different varieties of fish, you can still make a wonderful dish with just one or two. Get your fishmonger to scale, gut and fillet the fish, keeping all of the heads and bones for you.

FOR 6

2.5KG (5LB 8OZ) FILLETED MIXED ROCKFISH, MONKFISH, SCORPION FISH, JOHN DORY, SEA BREAM, GURNARD (IF YOU CAN); PLUS HEADS AND BONES

1 TSP SAFFRON THREADS

100ML (3½FL OZ) OLIVE OIL

SALT AND CAYENNE PEPPER

36 MUSSELS

12 LARGE TIGER PRAWNS

1 LARGE ONION, PEELED AND CHOPPED INTO DICE OF ABOUT 3CM (1¼IN)

1 LARGE FENNEL BULB, CHOPPED INTO DICE OF ABOUT 3CM (1¼IN)

6 GARLIC CLOVES, PEELED AND FINELY CHOPPED

2 PLUM TOMATOES, CHOPPED INTO DICE OF ABOUT 3CM (1¼IN)

1 LEVEL TBSP TOMATO CONCENTRATE

3 STRIPS DRIED ORANGE ZEST (SEE PAGE 173)

600G (1LB 5OZ) SMALL POTATOES, SCRUBBED AND THICKLY SLICED

To serve
1 quantity *Rouille* (see page 70-1)
croutons, sliced from a baguette, brushed with
  olive oil and baked until crisp

Preheat your oven to 190°C/375°F/Gas 5.
Check the fish for scales and remove if necessary. Cut the fish into even-sized pieces
and mix well with half the saffron and olive oil, and a good sprinkling of salt and
cayenne pepper. Set aside until needed.

Rinse the mussels in cold water then remove the beards from the bases of the shells
by pulling them upwards towards the fat part of the mussel and out. Any mussels that
may have opened, tap lightly and if they do not close, discard them. Halve the prawns
lengthways.

Sweat the onion, fennel, garlic and tomatoes in the remaining olive oil for 10 minutes
over a low heat until soft but not coloured. Raise the heat, add the tomato concentrate
and cook, stirring constantly, for a few minutes until it browns lightly. Add the fish
heads and bones, the remaining saffron and the orange zest. Cover with water, bring to
the boil and boil rapidly for 20 minutes, topping up the water if necessary. Strain bit
by bit, first of all through a colander, bashing the bones and shells with the back of a
ladle to extract every last bit of flavour. Taste, then reduce the broth a little if
necessary.

Salt the fish then lay it and the prawns flat on a couple of lipped oven trays. Pour over
some of the broth, and cook in the preheated oven for 10-15 minutes. At the same
time, cook the potatoes in a little of the broth and when they are almost cooked, add
the mussels, cover with a lid and boil quickly to open. (Discard any mussels that
remain closed.)

Strain the broth from the potatoes and mussels into the bulk of the broth, and bring to
the boil. Whisk about a third of it into half the *rouille*. Be sure to keep whisking until
the *rouille* is well combined and keep well away from the heat, as the egg in the
mixture will scramble if boiled. Pour the mussels and potatoes into a big warmed dish,
top with the fish and serve with the broth, remaining *rouille* and croûtons.

BOURRIDE DE LOTTE
Monkfish Bourride

Perhaps less known than bouillabaisse but nonetheless just as difficult to pronounce and a real Provençal classic. Thickened with a garlicky aïoli which is itself enriched with extra egg yolks, the finished soup has a velvet-smooth texture. The favoured fish for bourride are monkfish, John Dory and whiting. I think it is best, though, just using good meaty monkfish, which holds wonderfully and doesn't dry out while being poached.

Have your fishmonger fillet and trim the monkfish for you, keeping all the bones and trimmings for the stock.

FOR 4

1KG (2LB 4OZ) MONKFISH TAIL
1 LEEK, FINELY SLICED
1 ONION, PEELED AND FINELY SLICED
1 SMALL FENNEL BULB, FINELY SLICED
4 GARLIC CLOVES, PEELED AND SLICED
1 BOUQUET GARNI (THYME, BAY, DRIED ORANGE ZEST)
60ML (2¼FL OZ) OLIVE OIL
250ML (9FL OZ) DRY WHITE WINE
8 LARGE SLICES BAGUETTE, CUT AT AN ANGLE
2 EGG YOLKS
1 RECIPE AÏOLI (SEE PAGE 92)

PREHEAT YOUR OVEN TO 160°C/325°F/GAS 3.
Sweat the monkfish bones, leek, onion, fennel and bouquet garni in the olive oil for 5 minutes until soft. Pour over the white wine and boil off the alcohol. Add just enough water to cover, boil, skim, and simmer rapidly for 20 minutes.

In the meantime cut the monkfish fillets into slices at an angle. Try and get six thick even-sized slices per fillet. Set these aside.

Strain the stock and reduce it by about a third. (This part you can easily do well in advance.) Add the monkfish and gently poach it for about 10 minutes. While it is cooking toast the slices of bread in the oven until golden and crisp, and mix the egg yolks with half the aïoli in a large bowl. Put the rest of the aïoli in a serving dish.

When the monkfish is cooked lift it out on to the slices of bread and keep it warm in the oven. Boil the stock and add it little by little into the aïoli with the added egg yolks, whisking it in well and making sure it doesn't curdle. When you have added half of the stock, pour it back into the pot with the other half, stir well to combine and heat gently, making sure it doesn't boil.

Put the monkfish and toasted bread into four warmed soup plates, ladle over some of the soup, and serve the rest either in the pot or in a large tureen for people to help themselves. Offer the remaining aïoli on the side.

ROUILLE

There are as many versions of rouille *as there are for most Provençal recipes. Sometimes bread is used as a base, sometimes potato, but the only recurring ingredients are, of course, the olive oil and spice such as chilli or cayenne. You won't find mustard in any of these traditional recipes, but this just makes the* rouille *much easier to emulsify.*

MAKES ENOUGH FOR 1 RECIPE BOUILLABAISSE
$^1/_2$ RED PEPPER, SEEDED, ROASTED UNTIL SOFT (SEE PAGE 21) AND PUREED
1 TSP TOMATO CONCENTRATE
2 CLOVES GARLIC, PEELED AND CRUSHED
3 SMALL DRIED, NOT TOO SPICY CHILLIES, CRUMBLED, OR $^1/_4$ TSP CAYENNE PEPPER
1 LARGE EGG YOLK
1 TSP DIJON MUSTARD
150ML (5FL OZ) EXTRA VIRGIN OLIVE OIL
SALT

Reduce the puréed red pepper gently over heat with the tomato concentrate, crushed garlic and crumbled chilli until it becomes like a thick paste. Let it cool, then whisk it together with the egg yolk and mustard.

Pour in the olive oil, drip by drip, whisking continuously. When you've added about half like this without it separating, you can add the oil more quickly in a steady stream until emulsified. Season to taste.

If the *rouille* does separate, just mix another egg yolk with a teaspoon of mustard, then, whisking continuously, add the split mixture to it very slowly until it combines.

Soupe au Pistou
Vegetable Soup with Basil

This is the soup that inspired minestrone – just ask any Italian – but it's a vegetable soup by any name you like, with a great burst of basil at the end. I like to cook it very quickly and vary the vegetables, choosing whichever are freshest and best. You need not have as many varieties as I do: a couple from under and a few from above the ground will suffice.

Serving it one afternoon to some deeply rooted Provençaux, I explained with a grin how I deviated rather a lot from the traditional recipe: I used no pasta (they cringed),

I cooked it quickly (they frowned), but look, it's bright green (air was noisily sucked between varying amounts of teeth). A few shrugs later, when it was decided that I was young, therefore foolish and rash with plenty of time to see the error of my ways, they dipped their spoons. They all declared themselves famished when asking for seconds – no breakfast, lots of work today, etc... Allow a moment or two of smugness before serving.

For 6

1KG (2LB 4OZ) BORLOTTI BEANS, ABOUT 400G (14OZ) SHELLED WEIGHT (OPTIONAL)

2 SMALL LEEKS, WASHED AND FINELY SLICED

1 LARGE WHITE ONION, PEELED AND ROUGHLY CHOPPED

4 GARLIC CLOVES, PEELED AND SLICED

1 LARGE CARROT, PEELED AND CHOPPED

1 LARGE POTATO, PEELED AND CHOPPED

1 LARGE TURNIP, PEELED AND CHOPPED

6 TBSP OLIVE OIL

1 LARGE COURGETTE, DICED

1KG (2LB 4OZ) BROAD BEANS, ABOUT 300G (10½OZ) SHELLED WEIGHT, BLANCHED

250G (9OZ) FAT GREEN BEANS, BLANCHED AND CHOPPED

SALT AND FRESHLY GROUND BLACK PEPPER

4 TOMATOES, SEEDED AND DICED

100G (3½OZ) *PISTOU* (SEE PAGE 170)

First cook the borlotti beans well covered with water at slightly lower than simmering point for about 40 minutes until they are tender. In the meantime, sweat the leeks, onion, garlic, carrot, potato and turnip in a large shallow pan in the olive oil for 5 minutes or so. Cover with water, boil for 5 minutes, then add the courgettes and boil for another 5 minutes, topping up the water if necessary until the vegetables are soft. Add all the cooked beans and bring back to the boil. Season well, then finish with the tomato and pistou at the very last minute.

PETITS FARCIS PROVENCAUX
Provençal Stuffed Vegetables

These little vegetables, traditionally stuffed and baked with a mixture of minced pork and all sorts of aromatic goodies, get featured on menus all over Provence. As much as I love these, this lighter variation on the classic, with courgette purée and lashings of garlic, is perhaps an even better way of letting the roasted, slightly dried flavour of the tomatoes, peppers and courgettes come to the fore. I managed to get little round courgettes and tiny green peppers for the photograph overleaf, which were spectacular in both look and taste, but you can very easily cut larger ones down to size.

You can prepare all the vegetables well in advance and just sprinkle with the breadcrumbs and bake at the last minute.

FOR 4
4 VERY SMALL AUBERGINES
100ML (3½FL OZ) OLIVE OIL
JUICE OF 1 LEMON
8 SMALL TOMATOES
SALT AND FRESHLY GROUND BLACK PEPPER
4 BABY ARTICHOKES
2 ROUND COURGETTES
50G (1¾OZ) PROVENCAL BREADCRUMBS (SEE PAGE 31)
50G (1¾OZ) PARMESAN, FRESHLY GRATED

STUFFING
1 ONION, PEELED AND FINELY CHOPPED
4 GARLIC CLOVES, PEELED AND CHOPPED
3 TBSP OLIVE OIL
1 LARGE COURGETTE
1 SMALL BUNCH FRESH BASIL, LEAVES PICKED FROM THE STALKS

TO SERVE
800G (1LB 12OZ) RECIPE COOKED TOMATO SAUCE (SEE PAGE 167)

PREHEAT YOUR OVEN TO 180°C/350°F/GAS 4.
Remove the spiky bits at the top of the aubergines and cut them in half lengthways. Criss-cross the flesh side and brush them with 6 tablespoons of olive oil and half the lemon juice.

Slice a sliver off the bottom of the tomatoes so they sit flat and about a quarter off the top, using a serrated knife. Put them on a tray with the aubergines, drizzle with a little olive oil, season well with salt and black pepper and bake for 25 minutes, removing the tomatoes after 10. The aubergines should be totally soft inside.

Remove the tough outer leaves of the artichokes one by one until you get to the white centre. Trim the base to remove the bottoms of the green leaves and peel the tough outer layer of the stalk. Cook these at a brisk simmer in salted water with the remaining lemon juice for about 20 minutes until you can insert the blade of a small knife easily into the base of the artichoke. Leave these to cool in their own liquid, then halve and remove the chokes.

Cut the round courgettes into six wedges and blanch them in plenty of boiling salted water for 5 minutes. Refresh them quickly in iced water then drain and remove them as soon as they are cold. Remove the seedy centres (put these with the courgette for the stuffing) and reserve.

To make the stuffing sweat the onion and garlic in the olive oil for 5 minutes without colouring. Chop the courgette and seedy part from the round courgettes finely, then add to the pan. Cook this over a high heat for about 10 minutes, stirring frequently until the courgette is completely soft. Purée this mixture in the food processor with the basil leaves until fine. Season well with salt and pepper and reserve.

Spread some of the mixture over the aubergines, artichokes and courgette wedges. Lift the lids off the tomatoes and put a little on them, then put the tops back on. Sprinkle all with the breadcrumbs and Parmesan, then bake for about 10 minutes in the preheated oven until the crumbs are crisp. Serve with the hot tomato sauce.

PISSALADIERE
Caramelised Onion Tart

This is the pizza of Nice, and a rich creamy slice can be found at most street corners in the old town, in cafés, traiteurs *and even market caravans. Sweet from the onions, salty with the anchovies and oily from the olives, it's eaten warm, cold or straight from the oven. It's all in the onions: it is absolutely vital to soften them completely before you even consider caramelising them. If it takes a little longer than it says here, just wait: the soft, sweet, sticky mixture will be well worth it.*

FOR 4 GENEROUS STARTERS
ABOUT ½ RECIPE *FOUGASSE* DOUGH (SEE PAGE 182) OR PUFF PASTRY

TOPPING
1KG (2LB 4OZ) ONIONS, PEELED AND SLICED
6 LARGE GARLIC CLOVES, PEELED AND SLICED
100ML (3½FL OZ) OLIVE OIL
SALT AND CASTER SUGAR
15 SALTED ANCHOVY FILLETS, RINSED
15 BLACK OLIVES, HALVED AND STONED

PREHEAT YOUR OVEN TO 180°C/350°F/GAS 4.
Put the onion and garlic into a shallow pan with a tight-fitting lid with the olive oil, a teaspoon each of salt and sugar, and 100ml (1½fl oz) water. Cover the pan and cook the onions without colouring for about 10 minutes or more until completely soft and creamy. Take off the lid, turn up the heat and stand over the onions, stirring frequently, for 15 minutes or so until they are a dark caramel colour and the liquid has all but gone.

Roll out the *fougasse* dough or puff pastry to fit a 20cm (8in) tin. If you are using puff pastry, prick it well. Spread your onions evenly over this, decorate in a criss-cross or lattice design with the anchovies, then go around and fill the little holes with the olives. Bake the *pissaladière* for 20 minutes or so until the base is wonderfully crisp and the top is dark gold.

SALADE NICOISE

When done well, this is a delicious salad with more variations than I could ever keep up with. I looked through as many of those little old cookbooks as I could find in and around Nice, and the only one thing they all insisted on was that the vegetables should be fresh and raw. You can vary the selection. If I'd have found them on the day I would have added tiny young broad beans and fennel to this recipe. Most early recipes used salted anchovies rather than tuna, but if you must have it use some good quality (dolphin-friendly) tuna preserved in oil.

Always make too much salade Niçoise. *Let the leftovers have a good mingle overnight then find a good big, not too crusty, loaf in the morning. Slice off the top, hollow out about half of the insides then rub it all around with garlic. Moisten the inside very lightly with vinegar then spoon in your leftover* salade Niçoise. *Pour over some extra olive oil – 'go on, a little more' – then put the lid on top and press down well. Leave for a while for all the juices to soak into the bread, then cut into a highlight of Nice's street food, the* pan bagnat.

FOR 6 OR SO

4 LARGE TOMATOES

SALT AND FRESHLY GROUND BLACK PEPPER

4 EGGS

$^{1}/_{2}$ SMALL CUCUMBER

1 RED AND 1 GREEN PEPPER

6 SPRING ONIONS, OR A COUPLE OF SMALL RED ONIONS, PEELED

6 BABY ARTICHOKES

JUICE OF 2 LEMONS

2 GARLIC CLOVES, PEELED AND FINELY CHOPPED

100ML (3$^{1}/_{2}$FL OZ) BEST EXTRA VIRGIN OLIVE OIL

1 SMALL BUNCH FRESH BASIL, LEAVES PICKED FROM THE STALKS, SLICED

16 ANCHOVY FILLETS, IN OIL OR SALTED

100G (3$^{1}/_{2}$OZ)BLACK OLIVES, STONED

Core the tomatoes and cut them into quarters. If they are very large, cut into six pieces. Put them in a bowl, salt well and leave them for half an hour or so until all of the white juice runs out.

Bring a pot of water to the boil then gently place your eggs in and simmer them gently for 8 minutes. Drain them, but leave in the pan and run cold water over the top for about 5 minutes. Peel and halve or quarter them.

Seed the cucumber using a little spoon and cut the flesh in fine slices at a bit of an angle. Skin and seed the peppers and slice them and the spring onions not too finely. Remove the tough outer leaves from the artichokes and slice them as finely as you can. Mix them on their own with half the lemon juice.

Put the chopped garlic into a large salad bowl, then mix in the remaining lemon juice, some salt and pepper, about two-thirds of the olive oil and most of the basil. Drain the tomatoes, then add them along with the rest of the vegetables and give it all a gentle toss. At this stage I leave it for an hour or so to let everything soften and for the flavours to merge a little.

When you are ready, put your salad in a serving dish and top it with the halved eggs, anchovies and olives, scatter with a few leaves of basil and drizzle over the remaining olive oil.

AIOLI GARNI

Known as the 'golden butter' of Provence, this is a wonderful example of the type of food that is simple to make, and by being something that is shared around a table, inspires conversation, debate and very strong opinions and breath.

A purist would not be happy about my addition of mustard, my suggestion of using another oil apart from olive nor, I suppose, by the use of a whisk and bowl instead of the more traditional marble mortar and wooden pestle. I'm not flying in the face of tradition for the sake of it, but merely making sure that you succeed. The mustard helps emulsify the aïoli, for instance, and the whisk stops your arm falling off.

Make sure you have far too much: eating an aïoli should be done over hours.

MAKES ENOUGH FOR ABOUT 4

5-10 GARLIC CLOVES, PEELED
COARSE SEA SALT
2 FREE-RANGE EGG YOLKS
1 HEAPED TBSP DIJON MUSTARD
500ML (18FL OZ) EXTRA VIRGIN OLIVE OIL, NOT PEPPERY, OR $\frac{1}{2}$ VEGETABLE $\frac{1}{2}$ OLIVE

TO SERVE

COOKED PRAWNS
HARD-BOILED EGGS
COOKED SALT COD FLAKES
CAULIFLOWER FLORETS
BOILED POTATOES
ARTICHOKES
GREEN BEANS, RUNNERS
MUSSELS
BEETROOT
BOILED CARROTS

Crush the garlic with a generous pinch of salt. Scrape it into a bowl with the egg yolks, mustard and 1 tablespoon water. Whisking constantly, add the oil very slowly at first; then, as the emulsion begins, faster and faster. If the aïoli is too thick, add a little warm water.

Serve the aïoli on a large platter surrounded by all or some of the ingredients suggested, or a selection of crudités, or even just some good bread.

CHAPON DE MER FARCI
Stuffed Scorpion Fish

Chapon farci *is a great Provençal dish that I hope the adventurous among you will try. It is less well known than bouillabaisse or* bourride *only because of the scarcity of the fish and the cooks who can prepare it. For me,* chapon de mer – *which we know as scorpion fish – is unquestionably the greatest Mediterranean fish: the slightly spiny and actually dangerous orange-red exterior revealing exciting flesh that is as firm, pale and tender as can be. The taste and texture are said to be similar to that of capon, hence the name; but I disagree: it is unique. I have eaten* chapon *grilled simply with lemon and sage, roasted with artichokes and potatoes, and gently cooked in saffron and olive oil. All are wonderful, but braised, as here, in a stock slightly redolent of bouillabaisse that gains flavour with each gentle baste, it has no equal.*

FOR 4
1 LARGE SCORPION FISH, ABOUT 1.5KG (3LB 5OZ)
4 TIGER PRAWNS, PEELED (KEEP THE SHELLS FOR THE STOCK)
2 SMALL WHITE ONIONS, PEELED AND CHOPPED
4 GARLIC CLOVES, PEELED AND CHOPPED
1 SMALL RED PEPPER, SEEDED AND CHOPPED
50ML (2FL OZ) OLIVE OIL
1 TBSP TOMATO CONCENTRATE
100ML (3FL OZ) WHITE WINE
1 PINCH SAFFRON THREADS
100G (3½OZ) SWISS CHARD LEAVES (OR SPINACH OR ROCKET)
250G (9OZ) RECIPE *CONFIT DE TOMATES* (SEE PAGE 166), CHOPPED
50G (1¾OZ) DRIED BREADCRUMBS
8 SAGE LEAVES, FINELY SLICED
1 EGG YOLK
SALT AND CAYENNE PEPPER

TO SERVE
4 TBSP *ROUILLE* (SEE PAGE 77)

PREHEAT YOUR OVEN TO 180°C/350°F/GAS 4.
Cut off all of the fins then scale the *chapon*. Remove the central bone by cutting down each side of the backbone, stopping just before the tail and the head. With a pair of strong scissors cut through the bone just before the tail and the head. Empty the fish,

reserving the liver. Remove any pin bones with a pair of tweezers. Reserve all of the bones for the stock. Remove the black threads from the prawns, and chop the flesh.

Sweat the onion, garlic and red pepper in the olive oil for 5 minutes until soft. Separate this mixture into two and add the bones from the fish, the prawn shells and the tomato concentrate to one half. Fry for about 2 more minutes until the bones begin to caramelise, then add the white wine and reduce it by half. Cover with water, bring to the boil and boil for 15 minutes, topping up the water if necessary. Strain first of all through a colander, bashing the bones and shells with the back of a ladle to extract every last bit of flavour. Bring back to the boil, then strain through a fine sieve and add the saffron. It seems like a lot of trouble but you get more volume and flavour this way.

For the stuffing, slice the Swiss chard leaves, add them to the second half of the onion-garlic mixture and cook for 5 minutes until soft. Add the chopped prawns, *confit* tomatoes, breadcrumbs and sliced sage. Remove from the heat, add the egg yolk and season well with salt and cayenne.

Season the flesh of the *chapon*, and stuff it, pressing the mixture in well. Tie it up at least three times, then put the *chapon* in an ovenproof dish that just holds it. Pour over the stock, put in the preheated oven and braise, basting regularly, for 45 minutes. Check if it is ready by poking a skewer into the thickest part of the fish. If it comes out piping hot, the fish is ready.

Lift the *chapon* on to a warmed platter, cover it with foil and let it rest in a warm place for 15 minutes. Pour the stock into a saucepan, adding a little water to help scrape off any caramelised bits if necessary. Purée the reserved liver with a little of the stock and add it to the *rouille*.

Transfer the *chapon* to a chopping board, remove the string, present it to your guests to get them salivating, and return to the kitchen. First remove the head, scoop out the cheeks, and dip these in a little *rouille*. They are the best, most tender part, and yours as the spoils for taking so much effort. Bring the stock to the boil and keep hot.

With a very sharp, fine-bladed knife, cut through the middle of the fish, then across each fillet, which will give you four servings. Put each piece on top of the stuffing on a warmed plate. Whisk the *rouille* into the hot stock and make sure it doesn't come back to the boil. Season well and pour over the fish. Serve with plenty of basmati rice.

MORUE A LA BENEDICTINE (BRANDADE)
Salt Cod Purée

A completely traditional brandade *is just salt cod, garlic, olive oil and milk, but it is mostly served these days with mashed potato added. Legend has it that this recipe is so named after a monk, who was making a (potato-less)* brandade *for his fellow worshippers. All of a sudden there was a knock on the door and up turned a few fellows from a neighbouring monastery. The cheerful monk-cook did not panic. He put a great pot of potatoes on to boil, mashed them and added them to the fish, to the immense delight of his visitors who scraped their bowls and insisted on taking the recipe.*

FOR 4

600G (1LB 5OZ) SALT COD
4 LARGE GARLIC CLOVES, PEELED AND HALVED
1 BOUQUET GARNI
500G (1LB 2OZ) OLD WAXY POTATOES, PEELED AND CHOPPED
500G (1LB 2OZ) SMALL NEW POTATOES, SLICED 1CM ($^{1}/_{2}$IN) THICK AND PARBOILED
3 TBSP VEGETABLE OIL
250ML (9FL OZ) WHIPPING CREAM
125ML (4FL OZ) EXTRA VIRGIN OLIVE OIL
CAYENNE PEPPER
1 BUNCH FRESH PARSLEY, LEAVES PICKED FROM THE STALKS, SLICED

PREHEAT YOUR OVEN TO 180°C/350°F/GAS 4.

Sit the salt cod on a small rack then soak it in as big a container of water as you can muster, changing the water at least four times in 24 hours.

Give the cod a good rinse, put it in a pan that just holds it, cover it with water and add the garlic and bouquet garni. Bring it to the boil and simmer very gently for 20 minutes. While this is cooking boil the waxy potatoes until soft. Leave them in the hot water.

Once the cod is cooked pick out any bones and purée the flesh in the food processor. Strain and mash the potatoes then mix together with the cod in a saucepan.

Sauté the parboiled new potatoes until golden in the vegetable oil. Add the cream and olive oil to the *brandade* and season with a little cayenne. Toss the parsley through the sautéed potatoes, spread on top of the *brandade* and serve.

MORUE EN RAITE
Baked Salt Cod with Tomatoes, Olives and Capers

I am told this is a traditional Christmas Eve dish in the Var, our surrounding region. It is not a dish for the faint-hearted, with massive flavours that manage not to compete but combine. I have veered from the original recipe in cutting the cooking time for the sauce by about two-thirds and adding a little Parmesan cheese. Be warned, though, about the pungency of the fennel seeds when simmered: they certainly like to be noticed.

FOR 4
4 x 200G (7OZ) BONELESS PORTIONS OF SALT COD, SOAKED FOR 24 HOURS
2 TBSP VEGETABLE OIL
4 TBSP FRESHLY GRATED PARMESAN
3 LARGE SPRIGS FLAT-LEAF PARSLEY, LEAVES PICKED FROM THE STALKS, CHOPPED

SAUCE
1 SMALL ONION, PEELED AND DICED
4 GARLIC CLOVES, PEELED AND CRUSHED
2 TBSP OLIVE OIL
1 TSP PLAIN FLOUR
500ML (18FL OZ) RED WINE
500G (1LB 2OZ) CHOPPED TOMATOES (TINNED ARE FINE)
200ML (7FL OZ) WATER
1 BOUQUET GARNI (BAY, THYME, 3 STRIPS ORANGE ZEST)
1 PINCH FENNEL SEEDS
20 BLACK OLIVES, STONED AND CHOPPED
2 TBSP SMALL SALTED CAPERS, WELL RINSED
SALT AND CAYENNE PEPPER
CASTER SUGAR

PREHEAT YOUR OVEN TO 180°C/350°F/GAS 4.
Sweat the onion and garlic in the olive oil for 5 minutes until soft. Add the flour and stir for a minute or so to combine. Pour in the red wine and reduce by two-thirds, then add the tomatoes, water, bouquet garni and fennel seeds and simmer for 20 minutes until fairly thick. Strain through a sieve little by little, pressing well to extract the maximum of sauce. Add the olives and capers and season well with salt, sugar and cayenne. You will probably need plenty of sugar to balance the wine.

Fry the salt cod fillets for a few minutes each side in the vegetable oil until golden. Put them in an ovenproof dish, pour over the sauce, sprinkle with the Parmesan and parsley, and bake for 10 minutes. Serve immediately. Mashed potatoes made with olive oil instead of butter are a good accompaniment.

LOUP ROTI AU FENOUIL
Roast Sea Bass with Fennel

Sea bass and fennel make an adoring couple; you'll find them together on almost every menu across Provence. I have softened the combination here, blanching the fennel before roasting it with the sea bass. The semi-dried tomatoes add a little sweetener, and the blanched garlic a blissful finishing touch. The orange peel flavours the oil, which in turn flavours the sea bass as you baste it. If you are worried about filleting the fish once it is cooked you can make this using prepared fillets and halve the cooking time.

FOR 4
1 MEDIUM SEA BASS, 1KG (2LB 4OZ) OR OVER, SCALED AND GUTTED
2 LARGE FENNEL BULBS
A FEW DRIED FENNEL HERB BRANCHES (OPTIONAL)
250G (9OZ) RECIPE *CONFIT DE TOMATES* (SEE PAGE 166)
16 LARGE FRESH GARLIC CLOVES, BLANCHED IN 3 CHANGES OF WATER
12 STRIPS DRIED ORANGE ZEST (SEE PAGE 173)
100ML (3½FL OZ) OLIVE OIL
FLEUR DE SEL OR SEA SALT FLAKES AND COARSELY GROUND BLACK PEPPER
1 LEMON, CUT INTO WEDGES

PREHEAT YOUR OVEN TO 190°C/375°F/GAS 5.
Trim off any fronds remaining on the fennel bulbs and keep them to add to the branches. Remove any darkened bits from the outside of the bulbs and cut each one in six lengthways. Bring a large pot of salted water to the boil and blanch the fennel for around 10 minutes until you can pierce it easily with the blade of a small knife. Strain the fennel, dry it well and scatter it evenly across the base of a roasting pan with the fennel branches, tomatoes, garlic and orange zest.

Place the sea bass on top of the fennel and pour the olive oil over it and the vegetables. Sprinkle liberally with sea salt and pepper. Bake for 20 minutes in the preheated oven, basting it occasionally with the olive oil until the point of a knife comes out hot from the thickest part of the fish, near the head. Take the sea bass out of the oven and leave it in a warm place for 10 minutes to let it finish cooking.

Fillet the bass and remove as many of the little bones as possible. Serve it with the vegetables and cooking juices from the pan, the lemon wedges and either an olive oil-dressed green salad, or a ratatouille (see page 94).

La Daube Nicoise

Each region of France has its own version of daube, from boeuf bourguignon *to* boeuf bordelais. *In the Provençal version the addition of orange zest, tomato and, if you like, black olives, makes it stand out from the rest.*

This is a completely different way of marinating and cooking a daube than most of you will be used to. It is quicker and more practical than most recipes, and you really have to try it to experience the results for yourselves. The large pieces of beef are vital as there is more to caramelise, the darkened juicy outsides adding more flavour without drying. The hot wine penetrates more in an hour than cold, uncooked wine would in days, and nothing is added to the marinade so that you have nothing to scrape off when you have to fry the meat. The aromatics added to the pot will impart their flavour as much as is needed. One notable absentee is the bacon or coin de porc or anything of the like, which particularly if smoked just overpowers all the other flavours.

Having the oven at so low a temperature will cook the beef gently, below simmering point, so the finished dish is moist, tender and full of flavour. This is the secret: you can't cook a daube or stew too slowly, but at too high a temperature the beef will be tough and dry. If you don't have a saucepan to fry in and use in the oven, caramelise the pieces of beef first in a frying pan, then transfer them to a casserole, continuing afterwards in batches with all of the ingredients.

Don't make the daube on the day of eating: it keeps perfectly in the fridge for at least three days. Some say it tastes better the longer it is left, but I think this is probably because it's already made – you have a practically dish-free kitchen, but can still enjoy the wonderful aromas. When reheating, do so very slowly so the beef just warms through without toughening or drying out.

For 4

12 x 80-100g (3-3½oz) pieces of shin (or if you are really lucky, cheek) of beef

1 bottle robust red wine

50ml (2fl oz) groundnut oil

salt and freshly ground black pepper

30g (1¼oz) butter

16 large shallots, peeled

8 garlic cloves, peeled

1 heaped tbsp tomato concentrate

2 tomatoes, roughly chopped

2 heaped tbsp plain flour

30G (1¼OZ) DRIED CEPS
2 BAY LEAVES AND 2 SPRIGS FRESH THYME OR SAVORY TIED TOGETHER
4 STRIPS DRIED ORANGE ZEST (SEE PAGE 173)

TO FINISH
FINELY GRATED ZEST OF 1 ORANGE
2 LARGE RIPE TOMATOES, SEEDED AND DICED
12 LARGE BLACK OLIVES, STONED AND CHOPPED
3 LARGE SPRIGS FRESH SAVORY OR THYME, LEAVES PICKED FROM THE STALKS, CHOPPED

Put the chunks of beef into a bowl or container that just holds them. Reduce the wine by two-thirds as quickly as possible and pour over the beef. Cover and leave the beef to marinate for an hour or so, turning it occasionally.

PREHEAT YOUR OVEN TO 110°C/225°F/GAS ¼.
Pour the beef and marinade into a colander over a bowl and press to extract all the wine. Reserve the wine and dry the pieces of beef well on kitchen paper.

Heat the groundnut oil in a large ovenproof pan. Season the beef with salt then sear and colour in a single layer for 5 minutes. Do more than one batch if necessary. Add the butter then caramelise slowly for a further 5 minutes or so, never allowing the butter to burn and turning the beef occasionally so that it colours evenly.

Pour off half the fat, then add the shallots, garlic, tomato concentrate and tomatoes and cook over your highest heat for about 2 minutes until well browned. Spoon in the flour and stir well, then pour in the red wine marinade along with just enough water to cover. Bring to the boil and skim, add the dried ceps, bouquet garni and orange zest, then place into the preheated oven to braise for 3 hours, making absolutely sure that the liquid never boils. Check the meat: it should be tender, still moist and flaky enough to eat with a spoon. If not, just leave it to cook for a while longer. Be confident, it will happen.

Remove the beef from the oven, discard the bouquet garni and orange zest and gently, with a slotted spoon, transfer the beef, shallots and garlic to a tray in a single layer. Strain the cooking juices through a sieve into a clean saucepan. Reduce over a high heat by about a third until thick enough to coat the back of a spoon, and add the beef, shallots and garlic back to it. Season well; you'll probably need lots of sugar and black pepper to balance the wine. Sprinkle with the topping and serve.

CÔTES DE BOEUF AVEC OIGNONS ROUGES
Ribs of Beef with Red Onions and Garlic

France is a nation of carnivores, and the Provençaux are no exception. Steak and chips are eaten and loved here as much as any of the fish and vegetables. The favoured way of cooking ribs or any cut of beef is grilling them over vine trimmings outdoors. Although I enjoy the intense smoky flavour this gives the beef, I always miss the wonderful caramelised bits that get stuck to the bottom of the pan which make the base for a wonderful jus or, as here, flavoured butter. This is a garlic lovers' recipe so if it looks like being a little strong for your taste just halve the quantity.

FOR 4
2 WING RIBS OF BEEF, 1.25KG (2LB 12OZ)EACH
60G (2¼OZ) BEEF DRIPPING
100G (3½OZ) BUTTER
4 RED ONIONS, PEELED AND QUARTERED
8 GARLIC CLOVES, PEELED AND CRUSHED
1 LARGE BUNCH FLAT-LEAF PARSLEY, LEAVES PICKED FROM THE STALKS
SEA SALT AND FRESHLY GROUND BLACK PEPPER

PREHEAT YOUR OVEN TO 200°C/400°F/GAS 6.
Trim the ribs of beef, keeping any bits to help with the jus. Heat a large pan or roasting tray with the dripping. Season the ribs well and pan-fry them for a couple of minutes on each side, adding half the butter after a minute or so, until they are a wonderful golden brown.

Lift the ribs out on to a warmed plate and toss the quartered onions and any beef trimmings into the tray. Fry these for a few minutes, then put the ribs back in the pan along with any juices that have escaped and roast them in the preheated oven for about half an hour for medium rare, or a little longer for medium.

Take the ribs out and let them rest in a warm place for about 10 minutes, then add the remaining butter to the pan and scrape any caramelised juices off the bottom. Add the garlic and sweat it for a minute, then throw in the parsley leaves along with some salt and pepper. Stir all of this into the onions, carve the beef, and serve.

THE HUNT, THE HARVEST AND WINTER

The evenings shorten and it becomes cold at night. The leaves on the vines turn shades of red and gold, and a side of Provence that is less celebrated outside its boundaries begins. You can move around the markets more easily and wander into restaurants without booking. Cooking has different nuances: the excitement of the mushroom season starting and the game becoming available (officially). Fresh walnuts and chestnuts abound to crack and roast, and it all begins around the time of the grape harvest.

The harvest is a climax, finding out if another year's work – caring, pruning and worrying – is going to produce a wine worth drinking. Nervous talk is all of degrees of alcohol, tonnage and the weather. The weather is always of great concern in Provence and dominates conversations not in the polite, let's-pass-the-time way of the Anglo-Saxon, but in the passionate soothsayer's, always-right fashion of the Provençaux. It is only before and during the harvest when the grapes are at stake that I have heard anyone (quietly) doubt themselves.

There is a romantic vision that, for the uninitiated, accompanies the *vendange*. A blissful wander through the vines, secateurs in hand, sun on your face and the satisfying plop of heavy bunches of grapes falling into your basket. The air is sweet with the scent of the sun-gorged grapes bursting to become wine, and there is nowhere you would rather be. This sounds great but the reality of the pick is back-breaking, hard, sticky work during which any loss of concentration could quickly be accompanied by that of a finger.

Aches and blisters aside, the *vendange* is a time of great splendour with a multitude of festivals and feasts. Lunch, as always in France, is respected. A few hours are taken in the middle of the day to fill the belly and blood with enough energy to survive the afternoon and evening. When all is well in the vines and baskets are full, the alcohol is abundant and dinner is a happy event. Screams of laughter accompany boasts from those claiming to have picked the most.

Chosen dishes are the sort to be shared and grabbed at greedily from around the table. *Gigots* of slowly cooked lamb are served with garlicky beans – creamy cocos, both white and speckled, abundant, plump and soft. Fat ducks are smeared with thick dark honey and lemon and roasted with the first of the chestnuts. Great gratins of potatoes, chard, onions and aubergines are sliced and spooned gleefully on to plates. Soft cheeses will be baked with wine and garlic and eaten like fondues. The essence of the harvest is really captured in the desserts: tiny violet figs roasted with brown sugar, or simmered in sweet red wine; tarts and *clafoutis* made with deep purple autumn peaches known as *pêche de vigne*. After feasts like these and a day in the vines, sleep comes quickly and the anticipation of the end of the harvest hangs tantalizingly in the air.

Not long after the grape harvest comes a crop of another sort, the hunt for which is something of a national pastime all over France, and some of the richest pickings are to be had in Provence. In the main mushroom season, when rain is followed by sun, you'll come across cars parked in the most unusual places. These are usually far away from the spots where the mushrooms are actually found as these, once known, are jealously guarded. I've been left holding the basket and trying not to laugh during an impatient conversation between two, under other circumstances, good friends who stumbled across each other. It was hilarious. My friend gave vague directions which I knew were vague lies. He then started on the outright lies before grabbing me, my basket and the ceps, and leading me off in the wrong direction.

The variety of mushrooms to be found in the woods nearby is astonishing: hearty ceps, destined for sautés and grills, or to accompany roasted or grilled meats or fowl; the delicate girolles which I love to use in cream sauces, either for chicken or rabbit, but most lusciously over toasted, generously buttered brioche, or in omelettes; the *sanguine* which, when cut, bleeds bright orange and holds up perfectly to the Provençal treatment of garlic and parsley. If you are very lucky and you know someone who is in the know, you may come across what Sylvain, who as well as tending Peter's vines is a real man of the woods, calls the 'caviar of mushrooms': the exotic looking and delicious Caesar mushroom (*oronge* in French, or *amanites des Césars*). You also need to be with someone who is in the know because Caesar's sister is a poisonous toadstool (as are many in the Amanita family). The Caesar looks a little like an orange cep coming out of an egg and has a delicate flavour that needs either elegant or almost no accompaniment. I have sliced them raw into a salad with Parmesan and rocket. For simple perfection, I just grill them over a fierce heat and anoint them with fruity olive oil, salt and black pepper.

It's when the mushroom season overlaps with the hunt that the problems begin. Sylvain took the whole hunter-gatherer thing to a new level when he was shot in the backside while elatedly cutting the stalk of a fat cep. He was told that he was mistaken for a wild boar, an excuse which he accepted. However, I have my doubts. I think he rumbled someone's patch and this was just a warning. We take our fungi very seriously in Provence. The seasons are short and the rewards delightful.

The hunting season is less clearly defined. One can't help but notice that the chirping of late summer crickets is occasionally punctuated by gunshot. If we have guests, we try to sneeze or cough to cover the sound, and start to salivate at the prospect of another round of rich daubes, roasts and terrines. When embraced by Frenchmen, hunting really is an all-consuming passion. This passion was illustrated perfectly when a friend of ours, doing a spot of night hunting, fell asleep then fell out of the tree he was hiding in. Annoyed mainly because he might have frightened off an approaching *sanglier* or boar, he went straight back to his branch and stayed there until dawn. The next day he found out he'd broken three ribs but, undeterred, that night he was back in his tree.

There are some rare delights at this time of year. Fat partridges, hung for a week after shooting, then roasted with sweetly caramelised onions and served with creamy lentils and bacon. The now rare and wonderful woodcock is trussed with its beak, and roasted whole to be served on huge toasts spread with a hot pâté made with its livers and foie gras, then glazed with the pan juices enriched with cognac. The most popular offering is the wild boar, the different cuts of which have their own use, making wonderful *terrines de campagne*, roasts and the celebrated daube. A daube of wild boar is a wonderful dish, gamey but not too much so. The delicate exchange of flavours during a cooking process of braising without drying out leaves you with meat soft enough to eat with a spoon but still moist, succulent and enshrouded in a deep rich sauce. The secret is all in the slow careful cooking (I know, I do go on about this, but it is so, so important) which, while rendering a tough piece of meat tender, still keeps it moist.

Many vegetables that you wouldn't usually associate with Provence appear in autumn and winter: watercress from Toulon, Jerusalem artichokes, endives, celeriac and huge shallots which are roasted gently until soft and sweet. The rich wonderful winter cuisine of Provence takes hold. Big pieces of beef are grilled or roasted, and butter is often used instead of the more usual olive oil. Chicken *pot au feu* is thickened with aïoli to make a warming stew and broth, pigeons are roasted with ceps. Winter is a release from the heat and bustle of the visitors that crowd the place at the height of the season. The clear crisp days of autumn when we look across a different landscape, and the chill winter evenings in front of an open fire, are just as welcome as the return of the summer will be.

Salade aux Amanites des Cesars
Caesar Mushroom Salad

As I've said, these are the finest of fine mushrooms, with a colour and taste that is unique. You could use ceps, or even girolles, instead. The first time I ate a salad like this was in Lugarno. I had never heard of Ceasar mushrooms before then and I've since been hooked by their vibrant appearance and delicate flavour. That night, which sits deliciously clear in my memory, I ordered a second plate of ouvoli *('little eggs' in Italian) and although the next course was juicy crustaceans cooked at an easy-scenting distance on a grill fired with vine embers, it had no chance that evening. Use a really fruity olive oil for this.*

FOR 4
200G (7OZ) CAESAR MUSHROOMS, CLEANED
SMALL BUNCH OF FRESH ROCKET, SLICED
50G (1¾OZ) PARMESAN, FRESHLY SHAVED
100ML (3½FL OZ) FRUITY OLIVE OIL
SEA SALT FLAKES AND FRESHLY GROUND BLACK PEPPER

Slice the Caesar mushrooms as finely as possible with a very sharp knife. Lay them around your plates and scatter over the sliced rocket and Parmesan. Drizzle over the olive oil, and season with the salt flakes and just a little pepper.

Cepes et Chataignes Sautes au Vin Rouge
Sautéed Ceps and Chestnuts with Red Wine Sauce

This is a wintry combination of some of the best local ingredients. If the whole cloves of garlic come as a surprise, let yourself be surprised, for after the repeated blanchings they become soft and melting and ooze into the rich sauce. The ceps shouldn't be washed; they just need their stalks peeled or scraped and the tops wiped with a damp cloth.

FOR 4
800G (1LB 12OZ) SMALL TIGHT CEPS, CLEANED AND HALVED
4 TBSP OLIVE OIL
20 COOKED CHESTNUTS
2 HEADS OF GARLIC, SPLIT INTO CLOVES,
    PEELED AND BLANCHED IN 3 CHANGES OF WATER
100G (3½OZ) BUTTER

1 SMALL BUNCH FRESH FLAT-LEAF PARSLEY, LEAVES PICKED FROM THE STALKS
SALT AND FRESHLY GROUND BLACK PEPPER
200ML (7FL OZ) RICH RED WINE
CASTER SUGAR

Heat your largest frying pan with the olive oil until it smokes, then toss in the ceps and fry them over the highest possible heat for about 5 minutes. Add the chestnuts and cooked garlic, then sauté for a couple more minutes. Add half the butter and let it foam and bubble, then toss in the parsley and give the lot a good stir. Season with salt and plenty of black pepper, and turn all of this into a warm container.

Pour the red wine into the pan and boil until it is almost totally reduced. Remove from the heat and stir in the remaining butter. Season with salt, pepper and some sugar and spoon it on to your plates with the ceps, chestnuts, garlic and parsley.

OMELETTE AUX GIROLLES
Girolle Omelette

There is no great mystery to a well-made omelette. First get the brightest yellow yolked fresh eggs; have a special non-stick or cast-iron pan; stand over it stirring all the time; and eat the omelette as soon as it's made. The centre should be just cooked and creamy, and the outside not too coloured.

Mushroom omelettes are revered in season all over Provence. Girolles make the most elegant filling, and ceps the heartiest. This is typical not only of the respect for the seasons in Provence, but the strong opinions of the Provençaux. One autumn morning in St Tropez I was picking through a box of girolles, as was a local woman. We chatted about what we were going to do. She said that she was going to make an omelette, and when I said I was going to do a clever little rabbit dish, she looked at me unbelievingly. 'No, no, you've got to make an omelette. Il faut...'

FOR 1
3 VERY FRESH EGGS
SALT AND FRESHLY GROUND BLACK PEPPER
LARGE KNOB OF BUTTER
GOOD HANDFUL, ABOUT 50-70G (1³⁄₄-2¹⁄₂OZ) GIROLLES,
    TRIMMED AND QUICKLY WASHED
FEW SPRIGS OF PARSLEY, LEAVES PICKED FROM THE STALKS, SLICED

Using a fork, mix the eggs well with some salt and pepper.

Heat a little frying pan with half the butter and sauté the girolles for a couple of minutes. Add the parsley, transfer to a small plate and keep warm.

Melt the remaining butter in the same pan and add the eggs. Stir well, pulling the mixture from top to bottom and side to side. When the mixture is too firm to stir any more and set around the edges, spoon in the girolles. Fold the omelette and turn it on to a warm plate. Eat immediately.

Pour the sauce into the roasting pan, scrape off all of the juices well, bring to the boil, then transfer to a small pan and reserve.

Heat a cast-iron griddle or frying pan with the last of the vegetable oil until smoking and cook the potatoes and ceps until golden. Toss in the butter and dried savory and season.

Depending on your preference, you can either serve the pigeons whole, making sure you have finger bowls and large napkins, or carve them. If carving, make sure the potatoes and ceps are kept hot (an oven with the door ajar is the best place). Remove all of the legs first and keep them warm on the plate where the pigeons were resting. Run a very sharp knife down each side of the breastbone of each pigeon then cut through the joint at the top. Keep the breasts warm on the hot plate as you go. Add any escaped juices to the sauce, bring it to the boil and serve over the pigeon, ceps and potatoes.

ON ROASTING SMALL BIRDS

To get a crisp golden skin on a pigeon or any other bird of a similar size, such as partridge, is a painstaking but worthwhile process. You need to turn the birds on to their breasts, thighs and finally tops in the pan, making sure that each surface is well caramelised. The great thing is that you can do all of this in advance, then have them ready – on their backs on a rack over a roasting tray – at room temperature and just add a few minutes to the final cooking time. The pigeons can be bought and the sauce made at least four days in advance.

CASSOULET

Cassoulet is not something that is ordinarily associated with Provence. Its origins lie slightly to the west, in Toulouse, but it's another dish that is eaten with gusto all over France. The generous addition of tomatoes and the little shins of lamb are a variation on a dish that I love. Often cooked in two parts, then combined, I find it more flavoursome and practical to cook everything together as one. The cassoulet *should just murmur, not simmer or boil, so that the beans will absorb the flavours more fully and the meats dry less. Puréeing some of the beans and adding them back makes for a wonderfully creamy result which contrasts perfectly with the crisp topping.*

FOR 6

2 SHANKS OF LAMB, ABOUT 350G (12OZ) EACH

3 TBSP DUCK FAT

400G (14OZ) DRIED WHITE HARICOT BEANS, SOAKED

1 LARGE ONION, PEELED AND DICED

4 GARLIC CLOVES, PEELED AND DICED

3 ROMA TOMATOES, CORED AND CHOPPED

1 TBSP TOMATO CONCENTRATE

1 x 400G (14OZ) PIECE GARLIC SAUSAGE

2 TOULON SAUSAGES, 200G (7OZ) EACH

1 x 250G (9OZ) PIECE OF GREEN BACON, SKIN REMOVED

1 BOUQUET GARNI (1 BAY LEAF, 1 SPRIG FRESH THYME)

2 DUCK *CONFIT* LEGS (SEE PAGE 174)

SALT AND FRESHLY GROUND BLACK PEPPER

100G (3½OZ) COARSE BREADCRUMBS

PREHEAT YOUR OVEN TO 110°/C225°F/GAS ¼.

Sauté the lamb shanks for about 10 minutes in the duck fat, first over a high and then a medium heat until golden. Add the drained beans, diced onion and garlic, and sweat these for about 5 minutes until well coated with the fat but not coloured. Add the tomatoes and tomato concentrate and boil furiously, stirring well until the tomato just begins to caramelise. Add the lamb shanks back to the beans along with the sausages and bacon. Cover just to the level with water and add the bouquet garni. Bring to the boil, cover and cook for 2 hours in the preheated oven, making sure that the liquid never boils.

BOURRIDE DE VOLAILLE
Poached Chicken with Aïoli

This is an easier to eat and probably moister version of poule au pot, *thickened at the last with aïoli to enrich and enliven the broth. It is important to cook the vegetables and different cuts of chicken at different times so that everything cooks just so. You will have plenty of the stock left over: you can either freeze it or make a simple soup the next day, adding a few leeks and potatoes.*

FOR 4

1 MEDIUM CHICKEN
2 LARGE ONIONS, PEELED AND QUARTERED
6 GARLIC CLOVES, PEELED
1 BOUQUET GARNI (2 BAY LEAVES, LARGE SPRIG FRESH THYME OR SAVORY)
4 SMALL LEEKS, TRIMMED AND WASHED
4 SMALL TURNIPS, PEELED AND HALVED
2 LARGE CARROTS, PEELED AND HALVED
½ RECIPE AÏOLI (SEE PAGE 92)
SALT AND FRESHLY GROUND BLACK PEPPER
1 BUNCH FRESH CHIVES, CHOPPED

PREHEAT YOUR OVEN TO 180°C/350°F/GAS 4.
Portion the chicken, removing first the legs and then the breasts. Separate the legs into thigh and drumstick, and cut each breast in two widthways. Break the carcass in half and put it in a large deep pot, cover with water, bring to the boil and skim. Add the onions, garlic and bouquet garni and simmer for 45 minutes. Add the leeks, turnips and carrots and simmer for 15 minutes more. Add the chicken leg pieces and, after 20 minutes, the breast pieces. Lower the heat and cook at just under simmering point for a final 20 minutes.

While this is cooking, make the aïoli. Set aside in a cool place.

Remove and discard the carcass and the bouquet garni. Taste and season the stock. Pour 4 ladles of the stock into a smaller pan, boil it and then whisk it slowly into the aïoli as if making another mayonnaise. Be careful not to add it too quickly or it will separate. Add the chives to this sauce, and return to the small pan to keep warm, but do not re-boil. Lift the vegetables and chicken out of the unthickened stock, and serve in deep bowls covered with the aïoli-thickened broth.

CUISSES DE POULET BRAISEES AU VIN ROUGE
Braised Chicken Legs in Red Wine

The flavouring here echoes the orange- and herb-scented richness of the daubes. If you prefer, as Susan, our editor, suggested, rather than using the whole legs you can just use a couple of chicken thighs per person. This is easier as you don't have to butcher the legs. But at the time of the suggestion, we'd already taken the photo which we all really loved so we went with the original plan. Don't be tempted to use the breasts though; they just dry out instead of cooking to a melting moistness like the legs.

Once again, very slow careful cooking is the secret. Always give yourself plenty more time than the recipe says, as sometimes it will take a little longer. Never panic, the legs will always cook eventually. Cooking dinner once for fourteen or so at Le Baou, they still weren't ready as I was serving the starter, but they got there, leaving plenty of time for chat and a few extra glasses between courses.

FOR 4

8 CHICKEN LEGS, SEPARATED INTO THIGH AND DRUMSTICK
1 BOTTLE FULL-BODIED RED WINE
SALT AND FRESHLY GROUND BLACK PEPPER
50ML (2FL OZ) GROUNDNUT OIL
30G (1¼OZ) BUTTER
8 GARLIC CLOVES, PEELED
24 SMALL SHALLOTS, PEELED
2 TOMATOES, ROUGHLY CHOPPED
2 TBSP PLAIN FLOUR
30G (1¼OZ) DRIED CEPS
1 BOUQUET GARNI (2 BAY LEAVES, 1 LARGE SPRIG
    DRIED THYME OR SAVORY)
2 STRIPS DRIED ORANGE ZEST (SEE PAGE 173)
CORNFLOUR (OPTIONAL)
CASTER SUGAR

TO FINISH (OPTIONAL)

FINELY GRATED ZEST OF 1 ORANGE
2 LARGE RIPE TOMATOES, SEEDED AND DICED
12 LARGE BLACK OLIVES, STONED AND CHOPPED
3 LARGE SPRIGS SAVORY OR THYME,
    LEAVES PICKED FROM THE STALKS, CHOPPED

SWEET PROVENCE

Desserts have a special place at Christmas in Provence, where thirteen of them are served as a culinary ode to Christ and his twelve apostles. Throughout Provence families have their own selection and, far from being elaborate concoctions, these mainly consist of dried fruits, nuts and nougat. Four of them, known as the four beggars, are always the same: golden sultanas represent the Dominican monks; hazelnuts the Augustine robes; almonds the bare-footed Carmelites; and dried figs the Franciscans. There are dates and chestnuts, and a mixture of fruits both fresh and candied. Fruit cheeses and pastes and sometimes fruits preserved during summer in brandy or eau-de-vie also feature. So do the sweet, oval-shaped candies known as *caissons* from Aix-en-Provence and the citrus-flavoured olive oil brioche known as *Pompe à l'huile. La Pompe* varies in name and some ingredients from region to region, and is regarded as an essential part of Christmas, traditionally arranged on straw trays in threes as a symbol of trinity.

The rest of the year round, dessert time in Provence is mainly a feast of fruit. With the exception of Friday which is our dessert day, the sweetness at lunchtime at Le Baou is always provided by bowls full of whatever is ripest: fat white and yellow peaches, nectarines and juicy apricots; teeth- and tablecloth-staining black cherries; or, later in the season, sweet greengages. When I cook with stone fruit I never blanch, skin or poach it, having realised after years of blindly doing this that unless you are to serve the fruit in the syrup that you cooked it in much of the flavour is lost. I'll now roast or bake it in the oven at a low temperature to concentrate the flavours and caramelise the natural sugars.

Berries of all sorts are another great highlight of living in Provence. During late spring, summer and early autumn, they taste so much of themselves that they need little or no adornment.

Sorbets made from any very ripe fruit are a fresh and perfect way to end a meal. I don't cook or skin any fruit for sorbets. I just purée it with sugar and lemon juice to taste, then strain it if necessary and freeze it straightaway.

Every book, like every person, has to have at least a little chocolate, and I'll always make desserts with it in the evenings at least twice a week, no matter where I am. Provence has never been sweeter.

TOURTE DE BLETTES
Swiss Chard Tart

A strange-sounding idea but one rooted deep in tradition. I first came across it in old Nice when I thought I'd just misunderstood what the waitress had told me. I was sent scuttling through my phrase book to little avail. I shouldn't have bothered. It was and is delicious. The peach is a modern addition, which I think works well. Although afternoon tea is not really a Niçois tradition, I think it is the perfect time for this tart.

FOR 6-8
500G (1LB 2OZ) PLAIN FLOUR
200G (7OZ) UNSALTED BUTTER
150G (5½OZ) CASTER SUGAR
2 EGGS, PLUS 2 EGG YOLKS

FILLING
1 SMALL BUNCH SWISS CHARD
50G (1¾OZ) PARMESAN, FRESHLY GRATED
2 EGGS
100G (3½OZ) CURRANTS
100G (3½OZ) RAISINS
100G (3½OZ) PINE NUTS
150G (5½OZ) SOFT BROWN SUGAR
2 TBSP OLIVE OIL
1 LARGE PEACH OR APPLE

Mix the flour with the butter and sugar by hand or in your food processor until it becomes sandy, then add the whole eggs and a little water to bind. Knead the mixture then separate it into two-thirds and one-third. Pat each into a flat circle and put in the fridge to 'harden' for about an hour.

During this time remove and discard any of the base stalks of the Swiss chard. Separate the remaining stalks and leaves, and slice both as finely as possible. Rinse thoroughly and dry very well between two tea-towels. Mix with the rest of the filling ingredients except for the peach, and set aside.

PREHEAT YOUR OVEN TO 190°C/375°F/GAS 5.
Have ready a tart tin of about 20cm (8in) in diameter. Roll both pieces of pastry

between sheets of floured clingfilm. The round which is to be the base needs to be a lot larger than the tin, and the round for the lid just slightly larger than the tin. You will have far too much pastry, which makes it easier (freeze any trimmings for another use). When the pastry is rolled, put it in the fridge for 10 minutes before you use it. Line the tin with the larger piece of pastry, then spoon your Swiss chard mixture inside. Halve the peach and remove the stone. Slice the flesh and fan it around the top of the mixture. Wet the sides of the pastry a little, roll the second piece of pastry around your rolling pin, and gently roll it over the top. Seal the edges well, then remove any excess with a small knife.

Mix the 2 egg yolks with 2 tablespoons water, strain and then glaze the top of the pastry. Bake for about 30 minutes in the preheated oven until it is golden brown. Once cooked, transfer it to a cooling rack.

On Egg Washing
Using just the yolks, rather than the whole egg, achieves a perfect dark glaze. Adding a little water to this gets the texture right for a smooth glaze. The straining removes any bits of albumen which may be hanging about.

On Short Pastry
If you let short pastry cool in the fridge once it has been rolled you will have a much easier time shaping and cutting it.

On Tart Tins
The very best tart tin to have is one with no base – a ring, in effect – so that when your tart is cooked you just slide it off the sheet of silicone paper on the baking tray on to a rack and slip the ring off.

TARTE AUX PECHES
Peach Tart

This is an upside-down tart in the way of the tatin. *If you don't have a shallow pan of 20cm (8in) in diameter, you could make slightly more caramel and pour it into a tart tin.*

FOR 6
5 LARGE, SLIGHTLY UNDER-RIPE PEACHES (BUY 7 JUST IN CASE)
50G (1³/₄OZ) UNSALTED BUTTER
100G (3¹/₂OZ) CASTER SUGAR
1 DISC PUFF PASTRY, 24CM DIAMETER X 1CM (9¹/₂IN X ¹/₂IN) THICK

PREHEAT YOUR OVEN TO 180°C/350°F/GAS 4.
First get a bowl of water ready, just large enough to sit the bottom of a 20cm (8in), heat- and ovenproof pan in. In this pan, melt the butter and caster sugar together. Cook this, stirring frequently, until you have a dark caramel. Don't worry if it looks like it has separated; once the peaches are in it will be fine. Being very careful, as it may spit, put the base of the pan immediately into the cold water to stop the caramel from cooking.

Cut the peaches in half and remove the stones. Cut eight of the halves in half again. Then, once the caramel has cooled, lay the quarters around the outside of the pan to make a circle. Put the two halves, one on top of each other in the centre and push down well. The fruit should be as tightly packed as possible so, if you can, add a little more. Cook over a gentle heat until the peaches begin to caramelise lightly.

Cover with the pastry disc, tucking it in around the inside edges. Bake for 20-25 minutes in the preheated oven until the pastry is dark brown and dry. Remove the tart from the oven and leave to cool down.

When cold, place the pan over a high heat to melt the caramel and, using the whole of your hand, twist the tart around the pan. Put a plate over the top and turn it upside down. If you want to reheat it, slice into portions while cold (this is much easier than hot) and reheat for about 10 minutes in a warm oven. Serve with some cinnamon ice-cream or a good dollop of crème fraîche.

TARTE AUX POMMES
Apple Tart

You'll find a tart like this everywhere you go in France, and an apple tart in most cookery books. Up until very recently, my favourite apple tart was tarte tatin, *but then I discovered this technique for pressing the apples down while they cook. The juices and caramel soak into the pastry, then gather up around the sides, making for a crisp and delicious base and an intensely flavoured topping. Granny Smiths are the best apples for this: they are very firm and have an acidity to balance the sweetness.*

FOR 6-8

500G (1LB 2OZ) PUFF PASTRY, ROLLED AND CUT INTO 1 x 30CM (12IN) ROUND

7 LARGE GRANNY SMITH APPLES, PEELED, CORED AND SLICED AS FINELY AS POSSIBLE

150G (5½OZ) BUTTER

350G (12OZ) CASTER SUGAR

PREHEAT YOUR OVEN TO 180°C/350°F/GAS 4.

Prick the round of puff pastry with a fork and put it either on a non-stick baking tray or a tray lined with parchment paper. Lay the slices of apple first around the outside, overlapping each by about half and using only the perfect slices. Put the trimmings to one side. Put the last slice of apple in each round underneath the first. All of the trimmings and ends, slide halfway underneath each round to hold it up. Continue in ever-decreasing circles until you reach the centre. Put little knobs of butter all over the tart and sprinkle with 250g (9oz) sugar.

Put a piece of silicone paper over the top of the tart (the thicker stuff used to line cake tins and trays are good for this) and another tray on top. Press down well and bake the tart with the tray on top for about 25 minutes. Lift the tart from the oven, remove the top tray and very gently peel off the paper. The apples should be cooked and there will be a lot of juice around the outside. Sprinkle with the remaining sugar. Bake for a further 15-20 minutes until well caramelised. Just lifting the tart a little, check that the base is cooked as well. Allow to cool for about 10 minutes before trying to remove the tart from its tray and serve either hot or at room temperature.

TARTE ORANGE ET CHOCOLAT
Chocolate, Orange and Pine Nut Tart

There's nothing really that links chocolate to Provence, but you've got to have a few chocolate desserts in any book... The pine nuts and orange are more typical and combine to balance the richness of this sticky, cooked chocolate mousse. The tart can be made a day or so in advance, kept in the fridge and cooked on the day of serving, so long as once it is cooked, it doesn't go back in the fridge.

FOR ABOUT 6

CHOCOLATE SHORTBREAD PASTRY

80G (3OZ) UNSALTED BUTTER

50G (1³/₄OZ) ICING SUGAR, PLUS EXTRA FOR DUSTING

1 EGG YOLK

80G (3OZ) PLAIN FLOUR, PLUS EXTRA FOR DUSTING

40G (1¹/₂OZ) COCOA POWDER

2 TBSP WATER

ORANGE ZEST AND SAUCE

4 ORANGES

200G (7OZ) CASTER SUGAR

SALT

FILLING AND TOPPING

75G (2³/₄OZ) CHOCOLATE, 72% COCOA SOLIDS, CHOPPED

50G (1³/₄OZ) UNSALTED BUTTER, DICED

4 EGGS, SEPARATED

50G (1³/₄OZ) CASTER SUGAR

40G (1¹/₂OZ) COCOA POWDER

50G (1³/₄OZ) PINE NUTS

For the chocolate shortbread pastry, mix all the ingredients together until totally smooth, either by hand or in the food processor. The mixture will seem very wet but don't worry, it's meant to be this way. Put plenty of flour on your hands and shape the mixture into a flat circle. Wrap it in clingfilm and put in the fridge for at least half an hour to harden before rolling.

CLAFOUTIS AUX FIGUES ET MYRTILLES
Fig and Blueberry Clafoutis

A clafoutis *is really just fruit lightly bound in a sweet crêpe batter. Traditionally it is always made with cherries, which bleed darkly into the batter. Indeed it would have been a cherry* clafoutis *on this very page if not for an American friend mentioning blueberry muffins and an abundance of figs one autumn. I prefer to have much more fruit than batter.*

FOR 6

500G (1LB 2OZ) PURPLE FIGS, HALVED
2 LARGE PUNNETS ABOUT 1KG (2LB 4OZ) BLUEBERRIES
50G (1³/₄OZ) BUTTER, PLUS EXTRA FOR THE DISH
75G (2³/₄OZ) CASTER SUGAR, PLUS EXTRA FOR THE DISH AND DUSTING
100ML (3¹/₂FL OZ) DOUBLE CREAM
5 EGGS, BEATEN
75G (2³/₄OZ) PLAIN FLOUR
FINELY GRATED ZEST OF 2 LEMONS
75G (2³/₄OZ) BUTTER, MELTED
CREME FRAICHE TO SERVE

PREHEAT YOUR OVEN TO 180°C/350°F/GAS 4.

Liberally butter a porcelain or earthenware dish just large enough to hold the figs and blueberries. Dust it well with sugar and set aside.

Melt the 50g (1³/₄oz) butter and sauté the figs for a couple of minutes. Add the berries, just to warm them through, and pour the whole lot into the sugared mould. Mix the double cream together with the eggs then sift in the flour. Add the 75g (2³/₄oz) sugar, the lemon zest and the melted butter and whisk well to combine, making sure that there are no lumps. Pour this mixture over the top of the figs and berries, then bake for 20-25 minutes in the preheated oven until the outside is set but the centre is just trembling slightly.

Heat your grill to its highest setting and sprinkle the *clafoutis* thickly with caster sugar. Grill until golden and serve hot, warm or at room temperature with plenty of crème fraîche.

Figues Poches dans leur Coulis de Mures
Figs in Blackberry Coulis

Figs and blackberries are one of my favourite pairings. This was going to be an accompaniment to a creamy lemon concoction, but seeing and tasting it on its own I thought it best left in simple perfection. I use the very dark autumn figs and wild blackberries whenever possible. It's delightful served as is, but feel free to add a good spoonful of vanilla ice-cream or a dollop of crème fraiche.

For 4
500g (1lb 2oz) blackberries
200ml (7fl oz) water
200g (7oz) caster sugar, or more to taste
10 purple figs, halved

Boil the blackberries together with the water and sugar for 3-4 minutes. Push through a sieve into a clean pan. Add the figs, bring back to the boil and simmer for a minute. Serve hot or cold.

MILLEFEUILLE AUX FRAISES A LA CREME DE CITRON
Strawberries and Lemon Curd with Filo Pastry

Lemons and berries are real symbols of Provence. The big, gnarled, untreated lemons have a tarty fresh look and flavour that perks you up enormously. As for the strawberries, in season, particularly when warm from the sun, they have a corruptingly decadent fragrance. I've combined the two here with a little crispy filo to make a dessert that has everything; sweet, sour and crisp.

Not only that, you can prepare it all at least 12 hours in advance and just assemble at the last minute.

FOR 4

4 SHEETS OF FILO PASTRY
50G (2OZ) UNSALTED BUTTER, MELTED
ICING SUGAR FOR DUSTING

LEMON CURD

1 LARGE EGG
1 LARGE EGG YOLK
FINELY GRATED ZEST AND JUICE OF 1 LEMON, ABOUT 50ML (2FL OZ) JUICE
50G (2OZ) ICING SUGAR
50G (2OZ) BUTTER

THE STRAWBERRIES

450G (1LB) STRAWBERRIES, STEMS REMOVED
100G (3½OZ) ICING SUGAR

PREHEAT YOUR OVEN TO 180°C/350°F/GAS 4.

Double up the sheets of filo pastry so that you have two rectangles of two layers. Brush them well with the melted butter. Cut six 12 x 6cm (4½ x 2½in) rectangles from the two large rectangles and put them flat on a baking tray. Dredge them with plenty of icing sugar and bake for 6-8 minutes until golden and caramelised on top. Store in a dry place.

To make the lemon curd mix the eggs and sugar in a thick-bottomed, stainless-steel saucepan. Add the lemon zest, juice and butter and whisk over a medium heat until it thickens to the texture of a thick custard. Transfer the curd to a bowl, put a piece of clingfilm directly on the surface to stop a skin forming and leave it to cool. This can easily be made two days in advance.

Cut 150g (5oz) of the strawberries into small pieces and put them into a saucepan with the icing sugar and 2 tbs water. Cook this over a low heat for a couple of minutes until the sugar dissolves. Turn up the heat and simmer for 5 minutes until thick. Leave it to cool for a while, then halve or quarter the remaining strawberries and toss them through it.

Build each *millefeuille,* first starting with a little lemon curd followed by a filo rectangle, more lemon curd, the strawberries then another filo rectangle. Repeat this once more then make the other three.

GRATIN DE FRUITS ROUGES
Red Fruit Gratin

The most wonderful berry gratin I've ever made was using maras des bois, *which are a cross between wild and cultivated strawberries. They have all the flavour of the wild at the same time as being fat and juicy. They never seem to have a long run in the markets, but when they are about you can find your way to them by following your nose. You can use any mixture of berries for this gratin. If they are not perfectly ripe, add some sugar with the Grand Marnier and macerate them for a while just to sweeten them and get them bleeding a little. Very ripe peaches, finely sliced, are also wonderful in combination with raspberries.*

For 4

300G (10½OZ) STRAWBERRIES, HULLED
300G (10½OZ) RASPBERRIES
DASH OF GRAND MARNIER

Sabayon

4 EGG YOLKS
125G (4½OZ) CASTER SUGAR
JUICE OF 1 LEMON
1 GELATINE LEAF (OPTIONAL), SOAKED IN COLD WATER AND SQUEEZED DRY
100ML (3½FL OZ) WHIPPING CREAM

Put the egg yolks for the *sabayon* with the sugar and lemon juice in a bowl over a pan of simmering water. If you've got an electric whisk, use it to start the *sabayon* as, although you probably get more volume with a balloon whisk, this is hard work and takes a while. Whisk the egg yolks until they double in volume and have thickened enough for you to make a figure 8 clearly with your whisk on the top of the mixture. Add the gelatine (if using) and keep whisking, away from the heat, until it has dissolved. Continue whisking until the mixture is completely cold.

Whip the cream and fold it gently into the *sabayon*. Refrigerate the mixture until you need it. This can be done a day in advance.

When you are ready to serve, toss the berries with the Grand Marnier. Leave to macerate for a few minutes. Put them either in four heatproof plates or one large dish (this is the most practical) and top them with the *sabayon*. Heat your grill to its highest setting and glaze the gratin for about 1 minute until golden but not too brown on top.

On Adding Gelatine

The addition of gelatine here is a bit of an old chef's trick, as it stops the mixture from separating.

On Gratins

Your grill needs to be as hot as can be to glaze the top as quickly as possible and just warm the *sabayon* through without it separating. As not all domestic grills get quite hot enough (I'm always being told this), the easiest thing to do is use a blow-torch.

POIRES ROTIES AUX CHATAIGNES ET CHOCOLAT
Roast Pears with Chestnuts and Chocolate

The warm pears and chestnuts with the chocolate sauce and chestnut cream make a great combination for winter. You could of course have just the pears with the sauce, but I think the chestnuts and cream make it into something really special. Both cooked chestnuts and purée are now widely available; the sweetened purée is a favourite breakfast spread all over France.

FOR 4
2 VERY RIPE COMICE OR WILLIAMS PEARS
200G (7OZ) WHOLE COOKED AND PEELED CHESTNUTS
2 TBSP MELTED BUTTER
4 TBSP LIQUID HONEY

CHOCOLATE SAUCE
150ML (5FL OZ) WATER
50G (1³/₄OZ) ICING SUGAR
40G (1¹/₂OZ) COCOA POWDER
50G (1³/₄OZ) 70% CHOCOLATE, GRATED

CHESTNUT CREAM
1 X 250G (9OZ) TIN SWEETENED CHESTNUT PUREE
100ML (3¹/₂FL OZ) DOUBLE CREAM

PREHEAT YOUR OVEN TO 190°C/375°F/GAS 5.
Halve and core the pears, then put them in an ovenproof pan with the chestnuts, butter and honey, and bake for 20 minutes in the preheated oven.

While these are cooking, bring the water for the chocolate sauce to the boil with the sugar and cocoa powder and simmer, stirring continuously, for 2 minutes. Remove from the heat, add the chocolate and stir until it melts completely.

Soften the chestnut purée by stirring, and mix in the double cream.

Serve the pears and chestnuts either warm or at room temperature on the chocolate sauce with the chestnut cream spooned over or on the side.

THE PROVENCAL PANTRY

A Provençal kitchen, like any other, has to have a well stocked pantry. I always refer to the recipes here as my stand-bys. Anyone who comes to the school at Le Baou d'Infer will be bombarded with ideas for things that will keep and enhance not just the odd dinner party but everyday cooking, too. To state the obvious, one should always have a few bags of good dry pasta, a box of risotto rice, some dried wild mushrooms, peppers and chillies. On the liquid side, there should be a bottle of good olive oil, maybe also some flavoured with chilli or lemon zest, and bottles of balsamic, red and white wine vinegar, as well as some wine and Cognac.

With a jar of *pistou* handy you have the potential to transform a massive range of dishes with very little effort. Almost any savoury preparation goes with *pistou*. Sardines or mackerel can be grilled and generously brushed with *pistou* right at the end of their cooking time. Grilled or baked aubergines can be drenched in olive oil, cooked to a soft creaminess and spread with some chopped tomatoes mixed with *pistou*. And after pan-frying lamb cutlets, just add a few spoonfuls of water to the pan to deglaze the wonderful roasting juices and stir in a spoonful of *pistou*. *Pistou* keeps well in the fridge, as do *anchoïade* and tapenade. These two can be spread on croûtons as a canapé, mixed with goat's cheese or mozzarella. They also make great informal starters as dips with fresh young vegetables.

In the freezer, a bag full of herb breadcrumbs, made with half parsley and a little savory or thyme and half bread, can perk up a variety of dishes. You can take a handful at a time and have a crispy coating for a piece of monkfish or cod, or a topping for the famous *tomates Provençales*. These are just tomatoes, well seasoned, grilled until they begin to burst, and topped with these fragrant crumbs before being grilled again until golden. I never use fresh bread for the crumbs, but dry any leftovers and keep them in an airtight box. Also from the freezer a concentrated cube of home-made chicken stock can be quickly turned into a soothing chicken broth. If a sauce you are making needs some beefing up, a little of this frozen stock will do wonders.

Both Dijon mustard and balsamic, white wine or red wine vinaigrettes can be made in large quantities. They keep for months stored away from the light in a jar with a tight-fitting lid. The tight-fitting lid is also necessary so you can give them a good shake before use. If you don't have to make these each time, a wonderfully dressed salad, either on its own or with some roasted or finely sliced raw vegetables (particularly if you have a little mixture of herbs to add) is a doddle, making a delightful, simple and fresh meal.

Dried orange peel, as you will notice throughout the recipes, is a much loved flavouring in Provence. I've only started using it in a tomato sauce over the last couple of years, and along with a little cayenne, it lifts the sauce to another level. It also gives an unmistakeable scent to Provençal stews and daubes, from chicken and beef to wild boar, as well as adding a delicately fruity and sweet touch to bouillabaisse. Try grinding up a little with some black pepper, salt flakes and dried thyme, savory or rosemary: this makes a magical seasoning for a fillet of sea bream or a slice of lamb once it is carved.

Although you obviously need to make it all at some stage, the idea of having a well stocked pantry is to eat well all the time. Instead of making a little when you need something, make a lot at one time and store it in your pantry, fridge or freezer. So then, when time is limited, the food you cook doesn't need to have any less flavour, but is put together from and enhanced by a selection of favourite and flavoursome preparations. I've even added a wine, some jams and some pâtés…

COMPOTE DE TOMATES
Tomato Compote

A tomato compote is better described as it is in French, as a fondue. A melting, rich, sweet mixture that will go wonderfully with pasta, grilled fish or lamb. I've used it with sardines and baked it with creamy, melting mozzarella on top of roasted aubergines or inside soft peppers. It is also immensely practical as you can use it immediately, keep it in the fridge for three days or more or freeze it. Unless you have super, fat, juicy, ripe tomatoes, use tinned.

MAKES ABOUT 250G (9OZ)

1 LARGE ONION, PEELED AND FINELY CHOPPED
4 GARLIC CLOVES, PEELED AND FINELY CHOPPED
4 TBSP OLIVE OIL
3 LARGE RIPE TOMATOES, CORED AND ROUGHLY CHOPPED
1 TBSP TOMATO CONCENTRATE
2 TBSP BALSAMIC VINEGAR
2 STRIPS DRIED ORANGE ZEST (SEE PAGE 173)
SALT AND FRESHLY GROUND BLACK PEPPER

Sweat the onion and garlic in the olive oil for 5 minutes until soft but not coloured. Add the tomatoes, tomato concentrate, balsamic vinegar and orange zest, and cook over a medium heat, stirring occasionally, for about 10 minutes until most of the liquid has evaporated. Season well and keep warm.

TAPENADE
Olive Pâté

Use either green or black olives, no problem; but whatever you do, don't use pre-stoned: get good quality. Serve the pâté on crisp toasts, grilled potatoes, as a dip with young vegetables, or on the red mullet fillets on page 53. It'll keep for ages in the fridge.

MAKES ABOUT 300G (10½OZ)

300G (10½OZ) BLACK OLIVES, STONED (ABOUT 250G/9OZ)

2 TBSP SALTED CAPERS, RINSED AND WELL DRAINED

2 ANCHOVIES

1 GARLIC CLOVE, PEELED AND CRUSHED

1 SPRIG SAVORY OR THYME, LEAVES PICKED FROM THE STALKS

4 TBSP OLIVE OIL

Put all the ingredients into the bowl of a food processor or blender and blend together for as long or as little as you like, depending on whether you prefer a chunky or fine texture.

ANCHOIADE
Anchovy and Garlic Purée

Anchoïade is a salty, creamy little thirst-stimulator that works its magic perfectly alongside tapenade and its accompaniments at aperitif time. I use the anchovies preserved in oil rather than in salt as is traditional. If eating anchovies on their own, though, I'd plump for the salted, quicky rinsed and tarted up with lemon.

MAKES 300G (10½OZ)

40 ANCHOVY FILLETS IN OIL

1 LARGE GARLIC CLOVE, PEELED

75ML (2½FL OZ) OLIVE OIL

2 LARGE SPRIGS SAVORY OR THYME, LEAVES PICKED FROM THE STALKS

Blend all of the ingredients together to the texture that you prefer, either chunky or fine.

Eat immediately or store in the fridge, covered with more oil for up to a month.

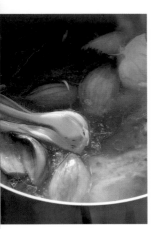

FOND BLANC DE VOLAILLE
Chicken Stock

This is a very simple fragrant chicken stock, quickly made and wonderful to drink just as a broth or use as a base for sauces and certain soups. You can make it using either fresh chicken carcasses or, even better, those that remain from a roast chicken as well as any sticky bits left in the roasting tray. If you like, you can add a bouquet garni of thyme and bay, and if it's a broth to beat winter that you want, just double the garlic. I prefer to let the true taste of the chicken sing out, which is why I omit the traditional mirepoix of carrot, celery and leek.

MAKES A LITRE (1¾ PINTS) OR SO
1KG (2LB 4OZ) CHICKEN BONES
2 ONIONS, PEELED AND ROUGHLY CHOPPED
6 GARLIC CLOVES, PEELED AND HALVED

Put the chicken bones into a large pan and cover them with cold water. Bring to the boil and skim well, then add the onions and garlic. Simmer for 2 hours, skimming only if necessary. You don't want to remove too much of the fat, as this will help the stock keep in the fridge (and can also be used for cooking). Strain the stock and it is ready to use.

If you want to freeze it, reduce it first by boiling (by about three-quarters) so it'll take up less space, then you can just add a little water when you want to use it.

ZESTES D'ORANGES SECHEES
Dried Orange Zest

Dried orange peel has been a gem of a discovery for me. It sits in a jar in my kitchen looking pretty unassuming, but just a few strips add a Provençal fragrance to any dish. It perks up bouillabaisse and, along with a few dried ceps, it is vital in a daube Niçoise, really making it stand out from those of Bordeaux or Burgundy. I'll certainly no longer entertain the thought of a cooked tomato dish without a few strips casting thier scent and spell.

PREHEAT YOUR OVEN TO AROUND 80°C/175°F/VERY LOW GAS.
Remove the zest but not pith of 5-6 large oranges in long strips using a vegetable peeler. Scatter the zest strips in a single layer on either a non-stick tray or a cake rack over a tray. Place into the preheated, very low oven, and leave for 6 hours (overnight is ideal), until they are dry enough to snap in your fingers. Allow to cool, then store in a sealed jar or an airtight box. They will keep for virtually forever, so long as the container is airtight.

VIN D'ORANGE
Orange Wine

This extremely popular aperitif is traditionally made with a mixture of sweet and bitter oranges, but it is lovely made with either alone, or with blood oranges or even lemons. I've given fairly large quantities to make it worthwhile, as it is best left for several weeks to mature. Serve very cold in small wine glasses.

MAKES ABOUT 2.5-3 LITRES
5 ORANGES
1 VANILLA POD, SPLIT AND SCRAPED
500G (1LB 2OZ) CASTER SUGAR
3 BOTTLES ROSÉ OR WHITE WINE
500ML (18FL OZ) EAU-DE-VIE OR VODKA

Wash then halve the oranges and slice them finely. Mix with the vanilla pod and sugar in a large non-reactive container with a lid, then pour over the wine and eau-de-vie. Stir well and cover, then keep in a cool dark place for four to six weeks, stirring from time to time. Strain through a muslin and bottle.

MOSAIQUE DE VOLAILLES
Duck and Chicken Terrine

This recipe is based on a terrine that I learned while working with Raymond Blanc. Although minus the foie gras he so loves, and slightly less extravagant than his, it still makes for a very elegant dish. The terrine is also extremely practical as it really should be made a few days in advance and will keep well in the fridge for up to five days. Serve with something sharp such as a few pickled vegetables or a well dressed salad and some grilled bread. You need a small terrine mould of about 15cm (6in).

FOR 6-8
2 LARGE CHICKEN BREASTS (ABOUT 175G/6OZ EACH)
1 LARGE DUCK BREAST
100G (3½OZ) CHICKEN LIVERS, TRIMMED, WELL RINSED AND DRIED
50ML (2FL OZ) COGNAC
1 LARGE SPRIG FRESH ROSEMARY, LEAVES PICKED FROM THE
    STALKS, FINELY CHOPPED
1 BAY LEAF
2 STRIPS DRIED ORANGE ZEST (SEE PAGE 173), GROUND
SALT AND FRESHLY GROUND BLACK PEPPER
VEGETABLE OIL FOR GREASING
10-12 PORK BACK FAT RASHERS TO LINE THE DISH

MOUSSE
100ML (3½FL OZ) RUBY PORT
50ML (2FL OZ) COGNAC
1 LARGE SHALLOT, PEELED AND FINELY CHOPPED
2 GARLIC CLOVES, PEELED AND FINELY CHOPPED
100G (3½OZ) CHICKEN LIVERS, TRIMMED, WELL RINSED AND DRIED
1 EGG, BEATEN
60G (2¼OZ) UNSALTED BUTTER, MELTED

PREHEAT YOUR OVEN TO 150°C/300°F/GAS 2.
Remove all sinews from the chicken breasts and just the top layer of fat from the duck. Slice each chicken breast into two and the duck breast into four. Remove any traces of green from the chicken livers and mix everything together with the Cognac, rosemary, bay leaf, orange zest and 1 teaspoon each of salt and pepper. Leave to marinate at room temperature while you prepare the rest.

Brush your terrine mould with a little oil and line first of all with a double layer
of non PVC clingfilm, followed by the back fat, making sure that you leave enough
of both overhanging to wrap the terrine afterwards. Set aside.

For the mousse, in a small saucepan, reduce the port and Cognac together with the
chopped shallot and garlic until almost dry. Purée this, then add the chicken livers
and process until the mixture is completely smooth. Add the egg and butter, purée
for a few more minutes until smooth and light and then strain the mousse mixture
through a sieve. Season well and keep at room temperature.

Pat the duck, chicken and livers dry with a little kitchen paper. Build the terrine by
putting in first a ladleful of the mousse to cover the bottom of the dish. Then place
on top one piece each of chicken and duck. Cover with another ladleful of mousse,
then another piece each of chicken and duck. Cover with mousse again, then all the
chicken livers. Layer up with the remaining chicken, duck and mousse, alternating
the position of the dark and light meats each time to create a mosaic effect.

Finish with the last of the mousse then fold first the back fat then the clingfilm over
the top. Cover with foil and cook and weight down exactly as for the *terrine de
campagne* on page 176.

CAILLETTES DU VAR
Liver and Bacon Sausages

Caillettes are specific to the Var, our département, and are found in most butchers and traiteurs. They also feature as a starter in many of the restaurants. Sometimes pork sweetbreads are used as well, although as these are very hard to get hold of, I have omitted them. A little nutmeg can be added which you may enjoy, or a good dash of eau-de-vie or marc. Be sure to roll the caillettes in their lovely cooking juices as they cool. The flavour is part roast and part bacon – you won't be able to resist licking your fingers afterwards.

FOR 6-8
1 LARGE PIECE CAUL FAT, ABOUT 200G (7OZ)
400G (14OZ) PORK LIVER
400G (14OZ) STREAKY BACON
100G (3½OZ) BACK FAT
1 BUNCH FRESH PARSLEY, LEAVES PICKED FROM THE STALKS, SLICED
3 GARLIC CLOVES, PEELED AND FINELY CHOPPED
5 SPRIGS DRIED THYME OR SAVORY, FINELY CRUMBLED
SALT AND FRESHLY GROUND BLACK PEPPER
3 TBSP VEGETABLE OIL

PREHEAT YOUR OVEN TO 170°C/340°F/GAS 3-4.
Rinse the caul fat under plenty of cold running water. Cut the liver into four long strips. Remove the outer skin from the streaky bacon and cut this into strips the same size. Cut the back fat into four thinner strips. Mix all of this with the parsley, garlic and savory. Season well.

Lay the caul fat out on a tea-towel and dry it well. Build up the meats on top of it, alternating the liver, bacon and back fat. Roll them up into a long sausage as tightly as you can inside the caul fat and trim off any excess. Tie it as you would a roast loin of pork.

Rub the outside with salt and pepper then place the roll in a dish that just holds it. Pour over the oil and roast in the preheated oven, basting occasionally for 45 minutes. Leave it to cool in its juices and keep it in the fridge for at least a day before serving.

LES CONFITURES DE PROVENCE
Provençal Jams

Here are four of my favourite and slightly more unusual fruit jams. I make them with preserving sugar to get a fresher flavour as you only need to cook them for 5-6 minutes. The method for all of them is essentially the same. I like to make them with the fruit chopped in large chunks, but if you like a more purée-like jam, feel free to chop them smaller. When I use berries, rather than mix and break them up, I prefer to give them a gentle toss with the sugar. Once the jams are cooked it is important to leave them in a bowl and to gently stir the fruit through from time to time so that it is evenly distributed before you bottle the jam.

All the recipes below make approximately 2kg (4½lb).

CONFITURE AUX FIGUES ET MURES
Fig and Blackberry Jam

600G (1LB 5OZ) PURPLE FIGS
400G (14OZ) BLACKBERRIES
1KG (2LB 4OZ) PRESERVING SUGAR
ROUGHLY GRATED ZEST AND JUICE OF 1 LEMON

Chop each fig into about six, then toss together with the blackberries, sugar, lemon zest and juice. Don't break up the blackberries. Allow the sugar to dissolve completely, then gently transfer the lot to a saucepan just slightly too large for the amount you have.

Gently bring the fruit mixture to the boil and boil for 6 minutes only, stirring occasionally and skimming off any scum that rises. Pour into a bowl and stir gently every now and then as it cools to distribute the fruit evenly. Bottle just before the jam has set.

CONFITURE AUX FRAMBOISES ET PIGNONS
Raspberry and Pine Nut Jam

1KG (2LB 4OZ) RASPBERRIES
1.1KG (2LB 8OZ) PRESERVING SUGAR
FINELY GRATED ZEST AND JUICE OF 1 ORANGE
200G (7OZ) PINE NUTS

Mix the fruit with the sugar, orange zest and juice, and proceed as on page 185.
Add the pine nuts after the jam is cooked. Pour into a bowl, stir and bottle.

CONFITURE DE PECHES BLANCHES ET BASILIC
White Peach and Basil Jam

1KG (2LB 4OZ) WHITE PEACHES OR NECTARINES (STONED WEIGHT),
    ABOUT 1.2KG (2LB 11OZ) BEFORE STONING
1KG (2LB 4OZ) PRESERVING SUGAR
FINELY GRATED ZEST AND JUICE OF 1 LEMON
1 SMALL BUNCH FRESH BASIL, LEAVES PICKED FROM THE STALKS, SLICED

Stone the peaches or nectarines, cut each half into six or eight, and proceed as
on page 185 with the sugar, lemon zest and lemon juice. Add the basil after the jam
is cooked. Pour the jam into a bowl, stir, and bottle.

CONFITURE D'ABRICOTS A LA VANILLE
Apricot and Vanilla Jam

1KG (2LB 4OZ) APRICOTS (STONED WEIGHT), ABOUT 1.3KG (3LB) BEFORE STONING
1KG (2LB 4OZ) PRESERVING SUGAR
FINELY GRATED ZEST OF 1 LEMON AND JUICE OF 2
1 LARGE MOIST VANILLA POD

Stone and chop the apricots and mix with the sugar, lemon zest and lemon juice.
Halve and scrape the vanilla pod and mix both the seeds and the pod with the apricots
and sugar. Proceed as on page 185. Pour into a bowl, stir and bottle.

INDEX

THE LEARNING CENTRE
HAMMERSMITH AND WEST
LONDON COLLEGE
GLIDDON ROAD
LONDON W14 9BL